this book belongs to:

me !

the next wave

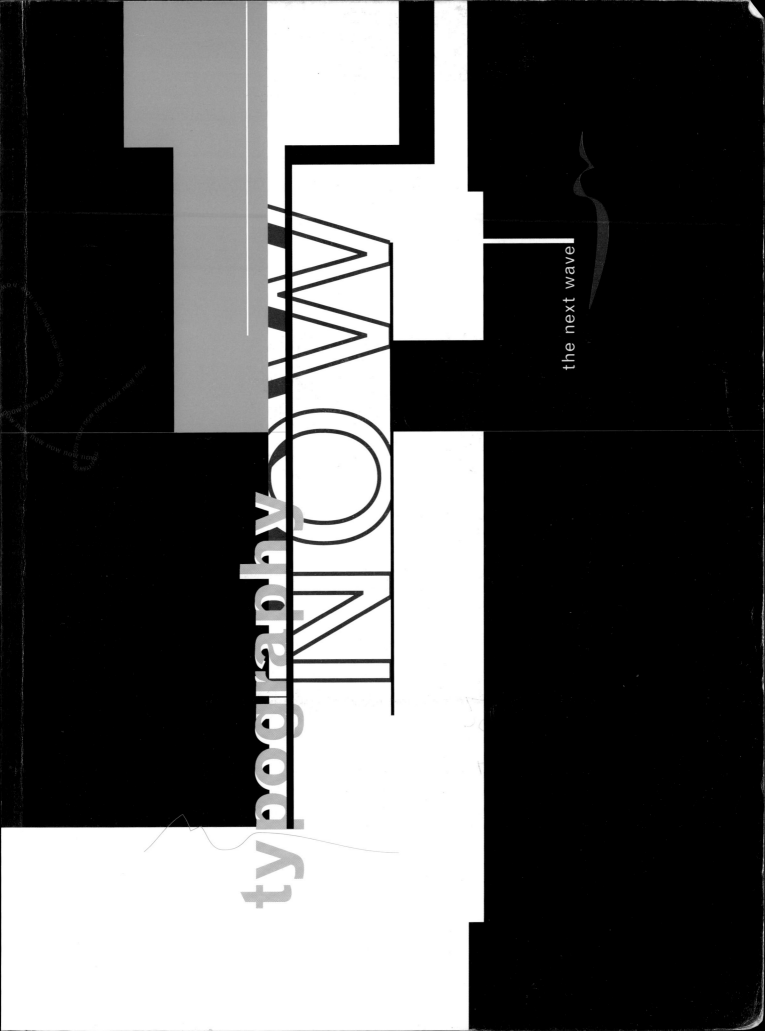

typography NOW

the next wave

edited by
**rick poynor
& edward booth-clibborn**

selected by
**rick poynor
& why not associates**

book design
why not associates

cover photograph by why not & rocco redondo.
end paper photography by pirco wolfframm & alistair lever.
computer-generated wave on cover by simon scott.
set in monotype grotesque by alphabet set.
printed and bound in hong kong by dai nippon printing

world rights: booth-clibborn editions, 12 percy street, london w1p 9fb.

isbn no. 1 873968 42 6

first published in 1991 by
booth-clibborn editions.
reprinted (three times) 1992.
reprinted 1993.
reprinted 1994.
first paperback edition 1994.
reprinted paperback 1995.
reprinted paperback 1997.
reprinted paperback 1998.
reprint paperback 2000

the typefaces beowolf,
brokenscript, lunatix,
oakland, matrix, modular,
scratch, totally gothic,
triplex and vortex were
kindly supplied by
fontworks, a division of
fontshop international.

type and deconstruction

in the digital era

by rick poynor

In the age of the desktop computer, font design software and page make-up programs, type has acquired a fluidity of physical outline, an ease of manipulation and, potentially, a lack of conceptual boundaries unimaginable only a few years ago. Everyone agrees that the new

digital tools

remove typography from the exclusive domain of the specialist – whether type designer, typefoundry or typesetting company – and place it (not always firmly) in the hands of the ordinary graphic designer. The results of this freedom, however, are the subject of intense and continuing debate. Traditionalists argue that the accessibility of the technology will accelerate the decline in typographic standards that started when the first clumsy photocomposition systems began to replace lead type. Evangelists enthuse about a soon to be realised

digital paradise

in which everyone will compose letters in personally configured typefaces as idiosyncratic as their own handwriting.

¶*Typography now: the next wave* is an interim report on these changes, filed while they are still under way. It collects new work – from America, Britain, Germany, France and The Netherlands – which is redefining our approach to typography. Some of these designs are entirely dependent on the new technology; in production terms it would be simply too time-consuming, costly or awkward to generate them in any other way. Some of them anticipate the aesthetic concerns of the new

digital typography,

or reflect the freedoms that the technology makes possible, while still being produced at the drawing board, or by letterpress. Some will stand the test of time; others will prove to have been representative of their period, but of no greater significance. All of them demonstrate their designers' reluctance to accept that the conventions of typography are inscribed inviolably on tablets of stone.

¶Among these articles of faith, legibility is perhaps the first and most emotive. If there is one characteristic that links the many visual strategies of the new typographers, it is their combined assault on this most sacred of cows. Swiss-school modernism composed orderly, linear, well-tempered messages using supposedly objective, and certainly inexpressive, sanserif letterforms. The new typographers, reacting against this bloodless neutrality, justify their experiments by arguing that

no typeface is inherently legible;

rather, in the words of type designer ZUZANA LICKO of Emigre Graphics,

"it is the reader's familiarity with faces that accounts for their legibility".[1]

We might find it impossible to read black letter with ease today, but in pre-war Germany it was the dominant letterform. Baskerville, rejected in 1757 as ugly and unreadable, is now regarded as one of the most serviceable typefaces for long text setting.

¶Type design in the

digital era

is quirky, personal and unreservedly subjective.

The **authoritarian voices of modernist typography,** which seem to permit only a single authorised reading, are rejected as too corporate, inflexible and limiting, as though typographic diversity itself might somehow re-enfranchise its readers.

"I think there are a lot of voices that have not been heard typographically,"

says Californian type designer JEFFERY KEEDY

"Whenever I start a new job and try to pick a typeface, none of the typefaces give me the voice that I need. They just don't relate to my experiences in my life. They're about somebody else's experiences, which don't belong to me."[2]

¶Another American type designer, BARRY DECK, speaks of trading in the

"myth of the transparency of typographical form for a more realistic attitude toward form, acknowledging that form carries meaning",[3] - - - - - - - - - - - - - - - -

1. "Do you read me?", *Emigre*, No.15, 1990, p.12.
2. *Emigre*, No.15, pp.16-17.
3. Designer's statement, August 1991.
4. *Emigre*, No.15, p.17.

The aim is to promote multiple rather than fixed readings, to provoke the reader into becoming an active participant in the construction

Of the message. Later modernist typography sought to reduce complexity and to clarify content, but the new typographers relish

ambiguity,

preferring the provisional utterance, alternative take and delayed punchline to the finely honed phrase.

"If someone interprets my work in a way that is totally new to me, I say fine,"

says Keedy. "That way your work has a life of its own.

You create a situation for people to do with it what they will, and you don't create an enclosed or encapsulated moment."[4]

Citizen Light
Citizen Bold

Zuzana Licko. Citizen typeface. 1990

as a designer i realized there is no escaping being post-modern, since the type-faces available are very old or are based on very old models. Even when you try to do something contemporary, you rely on these old typefaces and conventions.

Jeffery Keedy
Application of Keedy typeface
Emigre magazine, 1990

¶For Keedy, Deck, Emigre Graphics and colleagues such as NEVILLE BRODY and JONATHAN BARNBROOK in Britain, and MAX KISMAN in The Netherlands, designing typefaces for personal use is a way of ensuring that graphic design projects carry their own specific

identity

and tone of voice. The pre-digital typefaces that Brody drew for *The Face* emphasised the new perspectives on contemporary culture embodied in the magazine's editorial. They also functioned as a medium through which Brody could develop a socio-cultural

commentary

of his own. Typeface Two, designed in 1984, was deliberately authoritarian in mood, in order, Brody said, to draw a parallel between the social climate of the 1930s and 1980s. The typeface's geometric rigidity was persistently undermined by the light-hearted manner in which it was applied. Other designers take an even more idiosyncratic approach. For Barry Deck, the starting point for a type design is not traditional notions of legibility or elegance, but a highly subjective and seemingly arbitrary

narrative

founded on the supposed correlation between sexuality and letterforms.

Neville Brody
12" single cover
1984

Neville Brody
Typeface Two
1984

Neville Brody
Application of Typeface Two
The Face magazine, 1984

¶Fella, significantly, is a graduate of the Cranbrook Academy of Art,
the source of many of the most interesting developments in new typography.
Few Cranbrook exercises, however, are entirely typographic; the most typical
concentrate on the relationship of

image and text.

Cranbrook has been at the forefront in exploring the dense, complex

layering of elements

that is one of the most salient (and frequently criticised) characteristics of the
new typographic design. Unlike the earlier work of the New Wave designers, this
is not simply a formal exercise in collage-making; the method arises directly from

an engagement with content.

The Cranbrook theorists' aim, derived from French philosophy and literary
theory, is to

deconstruct,

or break apart and expose, the

manipulative visual language

and different levels of meaning embodied in a design, in the same way that
a literary critic might deconstruct and decode the verbal language of a novel.

6. *Emigre*, No.15, p.21.

7. "A brave new world: understanding deconstruction", *Print*, XLIV:VI, November/ December 1990, p.83. See also: Katherine McCoy and David Frej, "Typography as discourse", *ID*, Vol. 35 No. 2, 1988, p.34-37.

"When the deconstructionist approach is applied to design,"
write the American critics Chuck Byrne and Martha Witte,
"each layer, through the use of language and image, is an intentional performer in a deliberately playful game wherein the viewer can discover and experience the hidden complexities of language."[7]
The work that results (seen in this book in examples by KATHERINE McCOY,
ALLEN HORI and P. SCOTT MAKELA) is a direct challenge to its audience, which must
learn to "read" these layered, allusive, open-ended image/type constructions
with the same close attention that it would bring to a difficult piece of text.

Lisa Langhoff Vorhees,
Cranbrook Academy of Art
Concert poster
1990

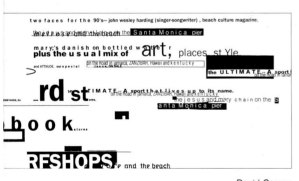

two faces for the 90's— john wesley harding (singer-songwriter) , beach culture magazine.

the jesus and mary chain on the Santa Monica pier

mary;'s danish on bottled water art, places st Yle
plus the usual mix of

and ATTITUDE. our special on the Road in Jamaica, ZANZIBAR, Hawaii and kentucky

the ULTIMATE: A sport

rd st ULTIMATE: A sport that lives up to its name.
on the road in Jamaica, ZANZIBAR, Hawaii and kentucky
the jesus and mary chain on the S
anta Monica pier

book stores

RESHOPS e and the beach

David Carson
Beach Culture magazine
1990

layering capabilities of the computer, are already widely dispersed.

The Californian surfing magazine *Beach Culture* rapidly became both *cause célèbre* and designer's *bête noire* for the deconstructive

frenzy

with which its art director, DAVID CARSON dismantled the typography of contents pages, headlines and text. In London, wHY NOT ASS OCIATES bring a similar typographic abandon to their catalogue dividers and covers for the clothing company Next. In each case the visual

delirium

is formally stunning, but its relevance to the content is not always clear. Both in their different ways are examples of what Andy Altmann of Why Not Associates calls

type as entertainment.

The designs function decoratively as a means of engaging, amusing, persuading and no doubt sometimes infuriating the reader, rather than as vehicles for extending meaning or exploring the text.

¶Such issues are unavoidable when it comes to the design of long pieces of prose. The questions of legibility and personal expression that preoccupy the new typographers become far more acute when the aim is to hold the reader's attention over the course of many pages. Are the new fonts

suitable for any purpose other than exotic display? Or is it time, perhaps, to re-examine the rigidly drawn distinction between typefaces for text and titles? Emigre Graphics, which is able to road-test its typefaces in its own magazine, has demonstrated the surprising readability of even the most bizarre and apparently

unpromising fonts,

given a little familiarity with their quirks. *Emigre*'s designer RUDy VANDERLANS mixes seemingly

incompatible faces,

varies point size and line depth, centres text over extra-wide measures, changes column width within articles, and runs two or more text-strands in parallel – most of the time

without

undue

loss of legibility.

Phil Baines
Postcard
1986

PHIL : J THING NG TO EARS C
anuary 1986. LO s *happening and w* lift a seven foot H *ompletion.* 5: (At
OKING ONE *ork being done, a* AIRY CIRCLE *last).* A *red, moun*
WAY, *pounds st good spirit.* 3: An *made of Silver Bir* tain BIKE, *lost fo*
erling; design as h dy Goldsworthy on ch. 25th January.' r *a moment,* IN S
igh street fashion Hampstead Heath 4: A Map of THE NOW *at 1100 fe*
as design. LOO , 'Very cold. Helpi CITY *of London n et, and rememberi*
KING ANOT *o develop my idea(ng the running I c*
HER, 1: Re the a *)s* .... DESIGNERS PLAYI *an no longer do:* '
bove, remembered
card from May 19 POSITIVE ROLE IN SOCI
84. (EXTRAC
T RIGHT) *at od*
ds but still an aspl .. I LIKE *that; it's a* t *is the caged taki*
ration. 2: Another *ng wing but it is n*
*term. Feels like an good st*ART. *ot space encompas*
other college with sed'. (K. Gibran).

¶But *Emigre* remains the exception. Most designers experimenting with radical approaches to page structure and typographic hierarchy work with a far more restricted and conventional selection of typefaces. The British typographer and letterpress exponent P H I L B A I N E S has turned to

medieval manuscripts,

Marshall McLuhan's *The Gutenberg galaxy,* concrete poetry and artists' books for

alternative models
of textual organisation.

Baines's autobiographical postcards and his undergraduate thesis, "The Bauhaus mistook legibility for communication", combine editorial rigour and sensitivity to language with a playful sense of typographic possibility.

"Legibility, presents information as facts rather than as experience,"[8] says Baines. There is nothing wrong with logic and linearity, he argues, but these qualities satisfy only the rational side of the brain. For Baines and his colleagues, it is equally important that typography should address our capacity for intuitive insight and simultaneous perception, and stimulate our senses as well as engaging our intellect.

¶Baines's most experimental work is still to be found in his personal projects, but in the last two years there have been a number of striking attempts to redefine the syntax of the conventional book. T I B O R K A L M A N 's catalogue for an exhibition about chaos theory and the arts subjects the essays to extremes of typographic distortion in an attempt to embody the exhibition's theme. In one essay, the word-spacing increases progressively until the

text disintegrates into particles;

in another, bold and under-sized characters are sprinkled randomly throughout the text. Avital Ronell's *The telephone book*, a discourse on the history, philosophy and psychoanalytical implications of the telephone, subverts the traditional elegance of a university press publication with a catalogue of

typographic mishaps

and metaphorical wrong numbers. Lines of type ripple with size changes, sections of text are crossed out or tilted at angles, whole pages are obscured by over-setting or

photographic erosion,

fragments of setting float free of the grid, and arguments break off and are never resumed. It is as though the entire book – a collaboration between "switchboard operator" Ronell, designer R I C H A R D E C K E R S L E Y and compositor Michael Jensen – is in the grip of some fiendish gremlin playing havoc with the telephone system.

8.
"The first consideration
of typography is to be
clearly read", debate,
Chartered Society of Designers,
London, 11 March 1991.

Wolfgang Weingart
Poster. 1977

¶Ambitious publishing projects such as *Emigre* and *The telephone book* suggest that the tradition of experimental typography initiated by Futurism, Dada and the Bauhaus, and sustained by the work of

ROBERT MASSIN
WOLFGANG WEINGART
WARREN LEHRER

and others, is still being refreshed. None of these projects is part of the typographic mainstream, or reaches a particularly wide readership, yet they are exerting an influence well beyond their milieu. The textual designs and many of the posters featured in *Typography now: the next wave* make large demands on their readers, but they make equally large demands on their designers. If this kind of typography is not to become simply an exercise in style, or fashionable deconstruction, then

Robert Massin
Page from Ionesco's play,
The bald prima donna

designers must be able to
function as visual editors

who can bring acute perception to their readings of the text. In some cases (*Emigre* and 8 v o 's magazine, *Octavo*, are examples) the designer might combine the role of editor and typographer. If this is not possible, then author and typographer must work together much more closely than is usually the case

**to establish
and amplify
textual meaning.**

Only then will there be a satisfying relationship between typographic expression and text.

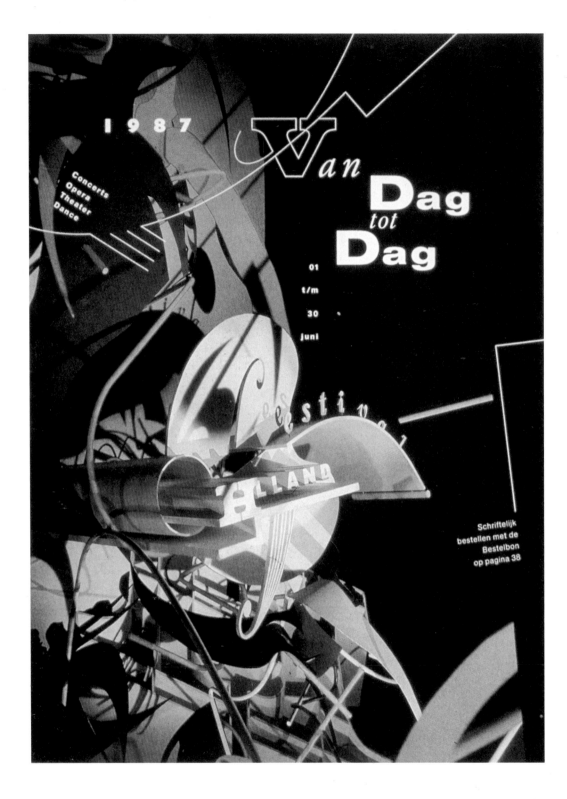

Van dag tot dag (From day to day). Festival magazine cover
Holland Festival, the Netherlands, 1987
Design Robert Nakata Studio Dumbar
Photography: Lex van Pieterson

Concertos for Orchestra. CD cover
Decca, UK, 1989
Design Nick Bell
Art director: Ann Bradbeer
Photography: Jim Friedman

Newsprint. Magazine cover. VRG
The Netherlands, 1990
Design Will de l'Ecluse
Ingeborg Bloem, UNA

left: *De voor-verkoop is al begonnen!*
(The pre-sale has begun!)
Poster. Holland Festival, The Netherlands, 1988
Design Vincent van Baar, Hans Meijboom
Studio Dumbar
Photography: Lex van Pieterson

below: Farewell party invitation. Rijksmuseum,
The Netherlands, 1989
Design Eric Nuyten
Studio Dumbar

opposite: *Programme 1987*. Cover
Holland Festival, The Netherlands, 1987
Design Robert Nakata
Studio Dumbar
Photography: Lex van Pieterson

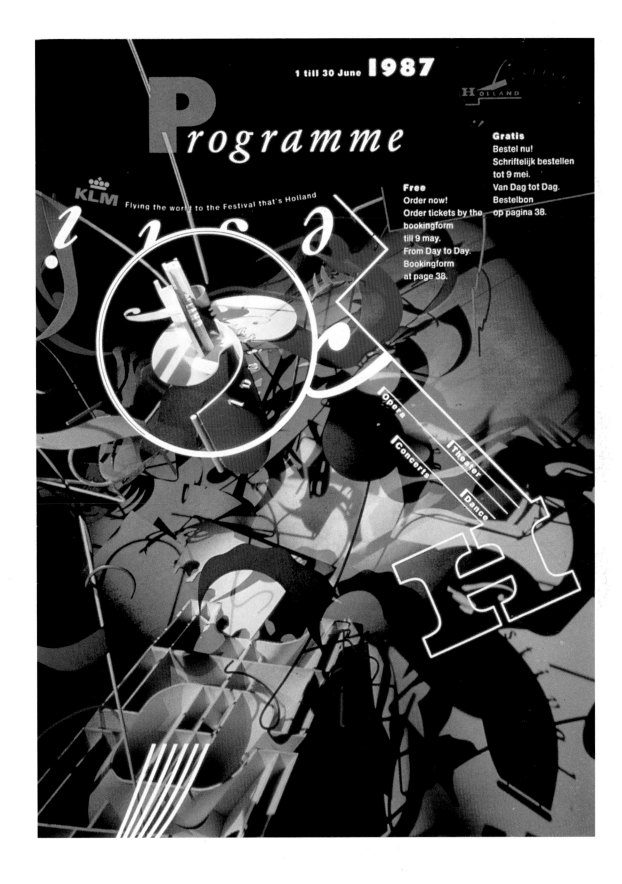

1 till 30 June **1987**

Programme

KLM Flying the world to the Festival that's Holland

Free
Order now!
Order tickets by the bookingform till 9 may.
From Day to Day.
Bookingform at page 38.

Gratis
Bestel nu!
Schriftelijk bestellen tot 9 mei.
Van Dag tot Dag.
Bestelbon op pagina 38.

Opera
Concerts
Theater
Dance

Paper stories. Promotional poster
Zanders, Germany, 1990
Design Helene Bergmans
Ton van Bragt
Alan Chandler
Studio Dumbar
Illustration: Henk Bank
Photography: Lex van Pieterson

ANDERS

Papiergeschichten
Paper stories
Histoi

...chte vom papierweißen Schimmel mit
...an Kopf, der an den letzten

Z

Y

FUTURE

PROGRESS**ZUKUNFT**

X

W

V

P

GLOSS
BRILLANCE
GLANZ

Gloss·Glanz·Brillance·Brillantezza·Brillo·Brilho·Glans·Lustro·Feny·Structure·Parlak·Λαμπρότητα·Глянец·光沢·光澤·مطفي   ikonofix 170 g/m   **ZANDERS** Feinpapiere AG

von: Sechsfarben Offsetdruck/Six colour offset printing/Offset 6 couleurs

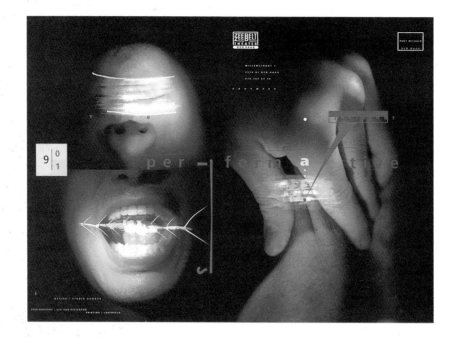

above: *Performative - Incision?*
Monthly mailer. Zeebelt Theatre,
The Netherlands, 1990
Design Allen Hori
Studio Dumbar
Photography: Lex van Pieterson

opposite: *Largo Desolato*. Poster
Bristol Old Vic, UK, 1986
Design Hans Bockting
Photography: Reinier Gerritsen

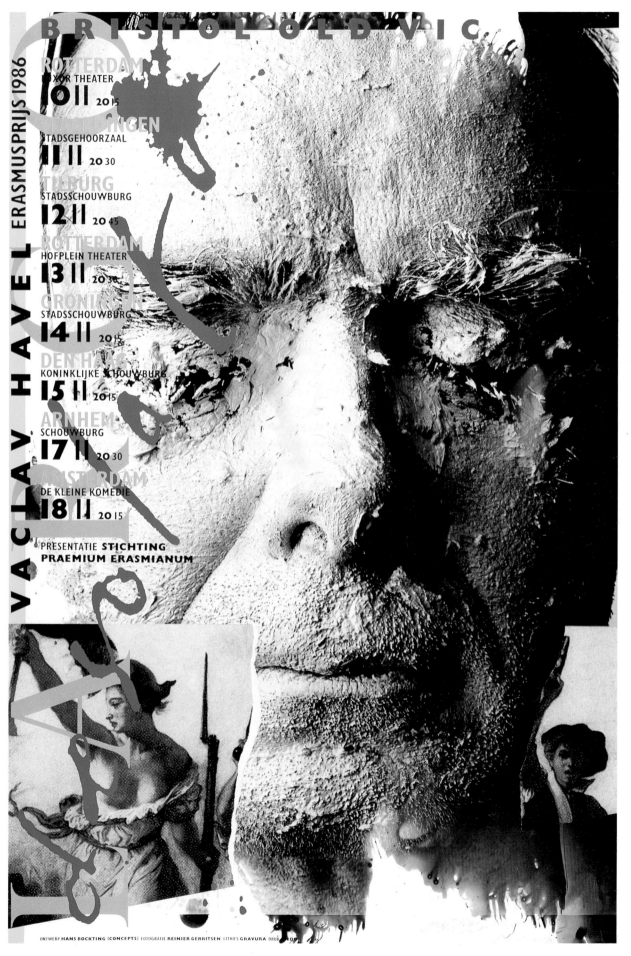

BRISTOL OLD VIC

ROTTERDAM
LUXOR THEATER
10 II 20 15

VLISSINGEN
STADSGEHOORZAAL
11 II 20 30

TILBURG
STADSSCHOUWBURG
12 II 20 45

ROTTERDAM
HOFPLEIN THEATER
13 II 20 30

GRONINGEN
STADSSCHOUWBURG
14 II 20 15

DEN HAAG
KONINKLIJKE SCHOUWBURG
15 II 20 15

ARNHEM
SCHOUWBURG
17 II 20 30

AMSTERDAM
DE KLEINE KOMEDIE
18 II 20 15

PRESENTATIE **STICHTING PRAEMIUM ERASMIANUM**

VACLAV HAVEL ERASMUSPRIJS 1986

ONTWERP HANS BOCKTING (CONCEPTS) FOTOGRAFIE REINIER GERRITSEN LITHO'S GRAVURA DRUK

Componist
david dramm

Toneelbeeld
edwin kolpa

Licht
marc van gelder

Kostuums
bianca van dillen

Choreografie
· phil griffin
· dries van der post en
· guido severien

dansproduktie

above: *Het Arsenaal/Dolf Stekhoven.* Posters
Icograda, The Netherlands, 1987
Design Armand Mevis, Linda van Deursen

opposite: *Tiga.* Poster. The Netherlands, 1990. Design Koweiden Postma
Photography: Hans Verschuuren

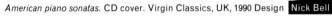

American piano sonatas. CD cover. Virgin Classics, UK, 1990 Design Nick Bell

Photography: Andy Rumball

Letterhead (back). UK, 1991
Design Nick Bell

Architects' brochure/poster
Daryl Jackson International, UK, 1990
Design Siobhan Keaney
Photography: Robert Shackleton

Brochure/mailer. King Tilly, UK, 1990

Design Siobhan Keaney

Photography: Robert Shackleton

Annual report. Cover. Apicorp, UK, 1988

Design Siobhan Keaney

Photography: Robert Shackleton

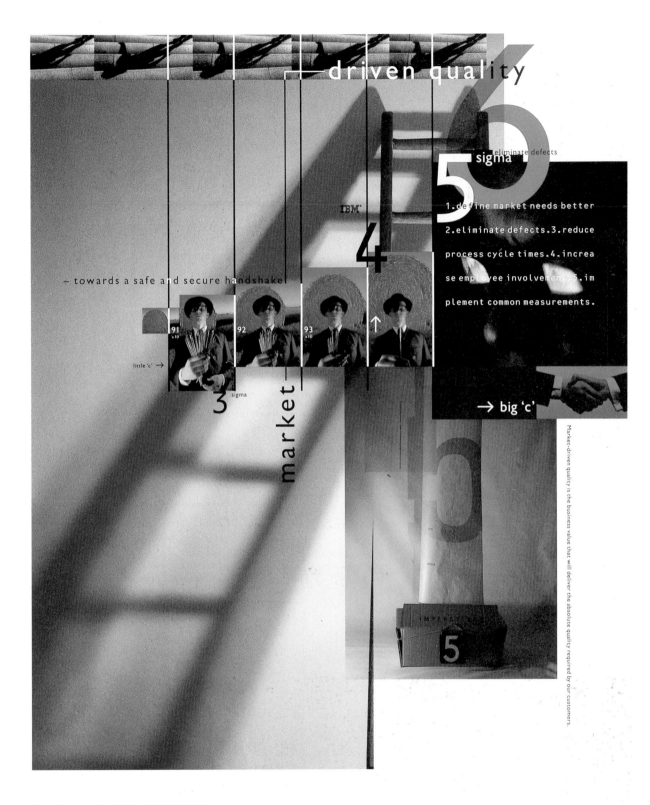

Annual review. Illustration. IBM, UK, 1991

Design Nick Bell

Photography: Andy Rumball, Nick Bell

Chinatown. Film poster. Germany, 1989
Hochschule für Gestaltung
Offenbach
Design Ines Blume

opposite: 1990 calendar. PTT, The Netherlands, 1989
Design Vorm Vijf

PTT RAC

De volledige verzorging van bedrijfswagenparken met 100% maatwerk

Onze **tijd** eist

op het gebied van de **beveiliging**

steeds betere p r e v e n t i e - maatregelen.

Dit geldt zeker voor waardetransporten,

maar in het algemeen voor e l k vervoer

dat de **PTT** iedere dag weer

voor de klant verzorgt.

De activiteiten van de PTT RAC

van gespecialiseerde voertuigen

ontwikkeling en bouw

onderhoud en herstel

van bedrijfsauto's

organisational lease

Ook n o o d z a a k leidt tot i n n o v a t i e

Inhoud, inzittenden en ook de

[luxe-bestel-vracht-] auto's zelf kunnen door

PTT RAC

optimaal worden beveiligd

door m i d d e l van:

versterkt g l a s

electrisch bediende p e n s l o t e n / g r e n d e l s

ontgrendelen met geheime c o d e s (key-free system)

op afstand starten en automatisch inschakelend a l a r m .

Dit communicatiemiddel,

waarbij de s a t e l l i e t centraal staat,

is van **GROOT** nut als mensen

geografisch v e r van elkaar verwijderd zijn.

Efficiënt en zakelijk vergaderen kan

met behulp van v i d e o c o n f e r e n c i n g

Deze nieuwe manier van vergaderen

bespaart fysieke inspanning,

tijd en geld

Er zijn ook andere toepassingen van beeldcommunicatie:

business-television,

1-zijdige beeldcommunicatie via een televisienet,

waarmee bijvoorbeeld een nieuw produkt

aan [een grote groep klanten **of**

werknemers van een bedrijf

met verschillende vestigingen getoond kan worden.

En er is **TELE** event:

a d h o c v i d e o v e r b i n d i n g e n

voor specifieke gebruikersgroepen

B E e c E o L m D m u n i c a t i e

betekent communicatie

tussen mensen maar op afstand

Beeldcommunicatie

met behulp van beeld en geluid

THEATRE DE L'
ATHÉNÉE
LOUIS JOUVET

PHEDRE

Du 12 mars au 20 avril 1991

DE MARINA TSVETAEVA
MISE EN SCENE:
SOPHIE
LOUCACHEVSKY

TRADUCTION: JEAN PIERRE MOREL
SCENOGRAPHIE ET COSTUMES: LOU COACO
LUMIERE: DOMINIQUE BRUGUIERE
MUSIQUE: ANNE MARIE FIJAL
AVEC:

YANN COLLETTE

ERIC DOYE

PHILIPPE FAURE

ANNE BENOIT

MICHELE GLEIZER

DOMINIQUE REYMOND

Avec le parrainage de

Union de Banques à Paris

Participation
Alpha Fnac

Phedre. Poster. Theatre de l'Athénée Louis Jouvet, France, 1991

Design Dirk
Behage
Pierre Bernard
Fokke Draaijer
Atelier de Création Graphique-Grapus

opposite: 1990 calendar. Poster. PTT, The Netherlands, 1990
Design Vorm Vijf

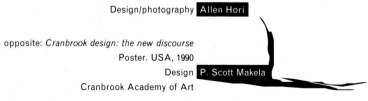

It feels like a bad play. Two-sided poster
Emigre Graphics, USA, 1989
Design/photography Allen Hori

opposite: *Cranbrook design: the new discourse*
Poster. USA, 1990
Design P. Scott Makela
Cranbrook Academy of Art

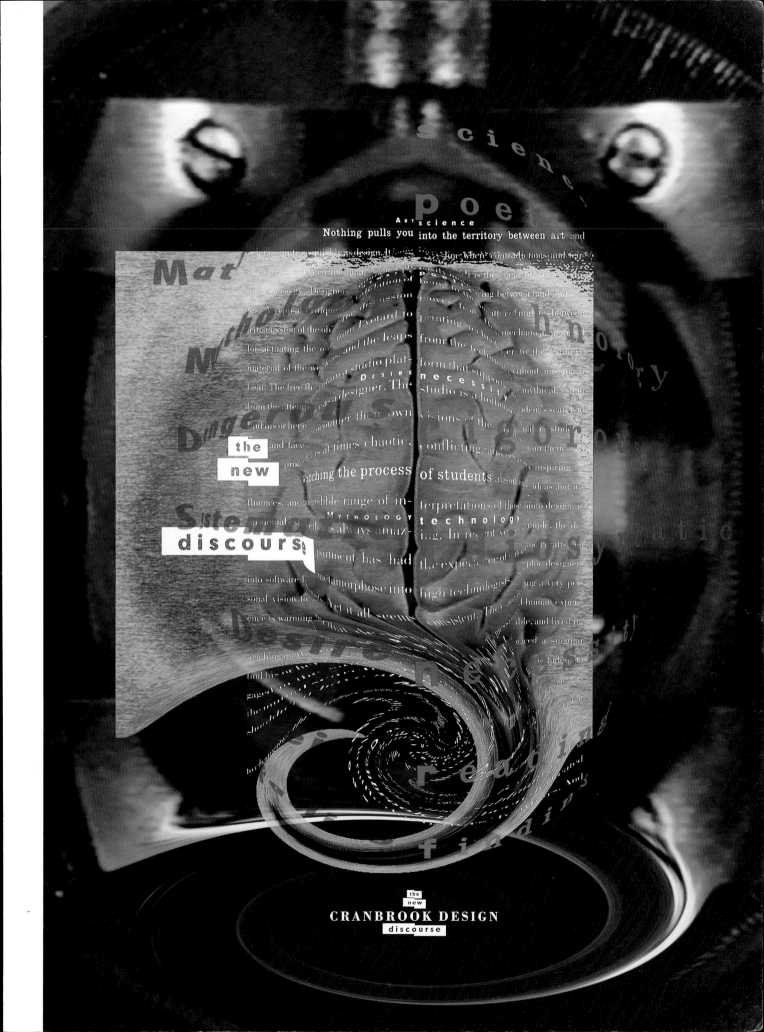

the
new
discourse

the
new
CRANBROOK DESIGN
discourse

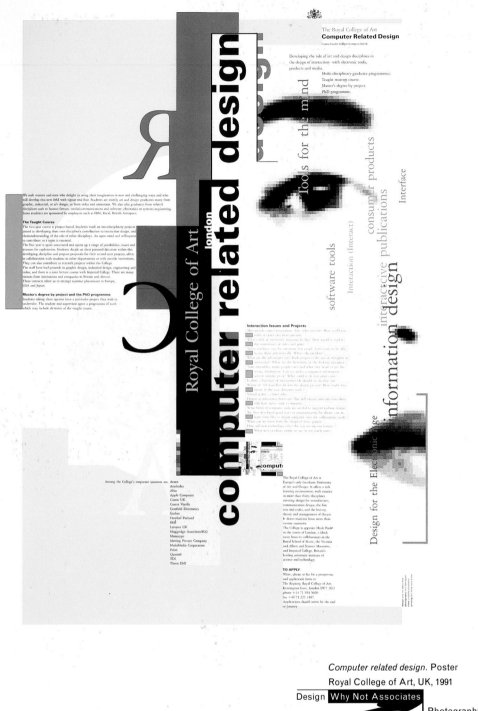

Computer related design. Poster
Royal College of Art, UK, 1991
Design Why Not Associates
Photography: Nick Harrington

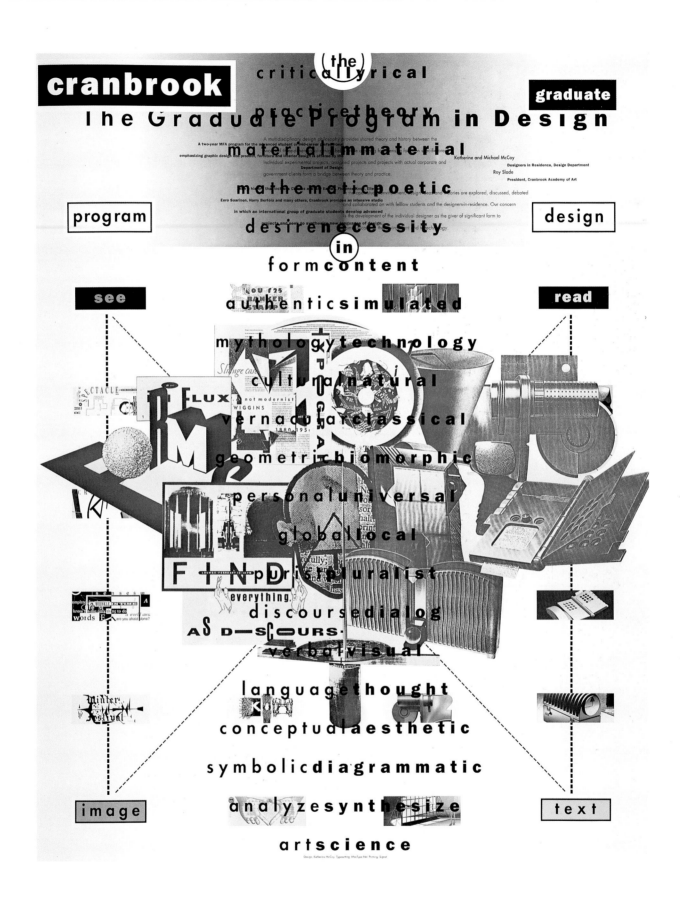

The Cranbrook graduate program in design. Poster
Cranbrook Academy of Art, USA, 1989
Design Katherine McCoy

Amnesty International. Poster. USA, 1991. Design Joan Dobkin Cranbrook Academy of Art

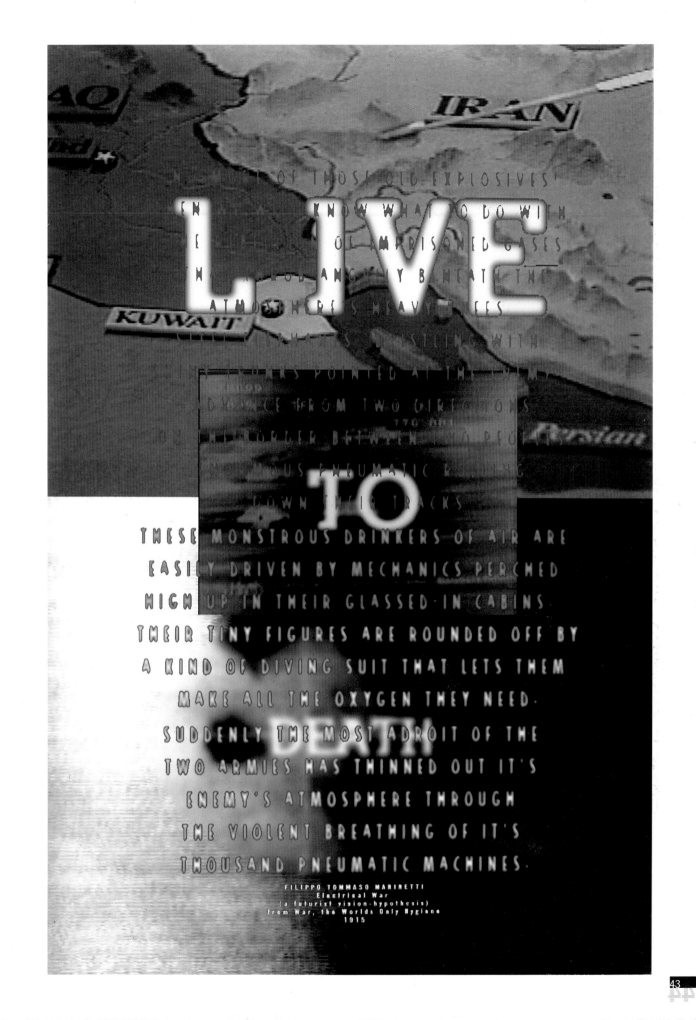

LIVE TO DEATH

THESE MONSTROUS DRINKERS OF AIR ARE
EASILY DRIVEN BY MECHANICS PERCHED
HIGH UP IN THEIR GLASSED-IN CABINS.
THEIR TINY FIGURES ARE ROUNDED OFF BY
A KIND OF DIVING SUIT THAT LETS THEM
MAKE ALL THE OXYGEN THEY NEED.
SUDDENLY THE MOST ADROIT OF THE
TWO ARMIES HAS THINNED OUT IT'S
ENEMY'S ATMOSPHERE THROUGH
THE VIOLENT BREATHING OF IT'S
THOUSAND PNEUMATIC MACHINES.

FILIPPO TOMMASO MARINETTI
Electrical War
(a futurist vision-hypothesis)
from War, the Worlds Only Hygiene
1915

Live to Death. Poster. USA, 1991. Design P. Scott Makela Cranbrook Academy of Art

Why Not Associates Graphic Design, Fotografie und Film

mit freundlicher Unterstützung des Deutsches Kommitees des Type Directors Club of New York

above: Exhibition invitation. UK, 1991
right: *Next Directory Preview*. Catalogue cover. Next, UK, 1991
Design Why Not Associates

Photography: Why Not Associates,
Rocco Redondo

Lamp/Feel. Poster. USA, 1991
Design Mark D. Sylvester
Cranbrook Academy of Art

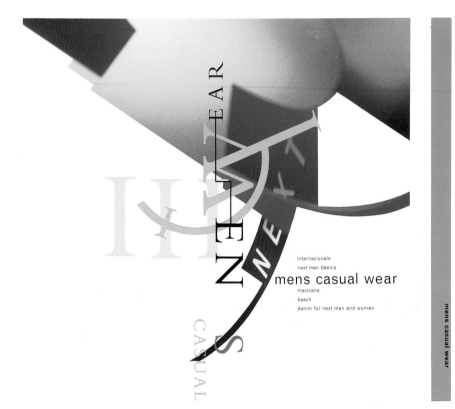

internazionale
next men basics
mens casual wear
mexicana
beach
denim for next men and women

mens casual wear

Next Directory 5. Section divider. Next, UK, 1990
Design Why Not Associates
Photography: Why Not Associates,
Rocco Redondo

opposite: *Morris Brose: a sustained vision*
Poster/mailer (front)
Detroit Focus Gallery, USA, 1987
Design Edward Fella

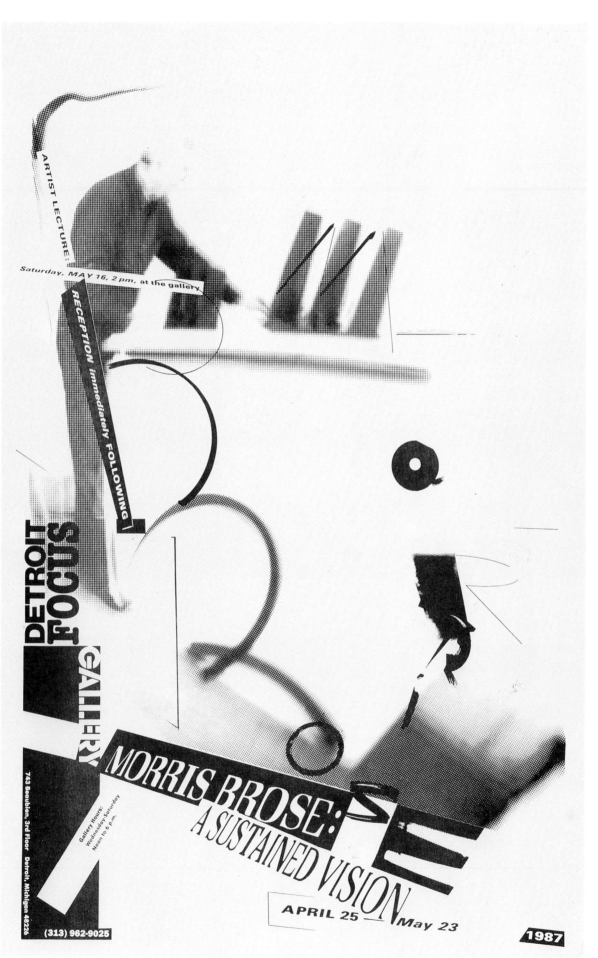

ARTIST LECTURE:

Saturday, MAY 16, 2 pm, at the gallery

RECEPTION immediately FOLLOWING

DETROIT FOCUS GALLERY

743 Beaubien, 3rd Floor
Detroit, Michigan 48226

Gallery Hours:
Wednesday-Saturday
Noon to 6 p.m.

(313) 962-9025

MORRIS BROSE:
A SUSTAINED VISION

APRIL 25 — May 23

1987

MORRIS BROSE:
A SUSTAINED VISION

(313) 962-9025

DETROIT FOCUS GALLERY

743 Beaubien Detroit Michigan 48226

APRIL 25 — May 23 1987

Design: Edward Fella, Cranbrook

With the support of the National Endowment for the Arts
the Michigan Council for the Arts
Detroit Council of the Arts

Non-profit Org.
Bulk Rate
U.S. Postage
PAID
DETROIT

Permit No. 2960

Promotional poster. Dwight Yaeger Typographer, USA, 1991
Design John Weber

opposite: *Morris Brose: a sustained vision*
Poster/mailer (back)
Detroit Focus Gallery, USA, 1987
Design Edward Fella

ᅮᅮ
ᅮ두
ARTSPACE

PrOpOsed
video GRANT

Hi8
V i d e o
Production *and*
Post-PRODUCTION
S u i t e
Residencies

San Francisco Artspace
announces a new grant program of-
fering artists access to video Hi8
equipment and audio facilities to
produce new works. Artists are encouraged to submit proposals describing their project idea and out-
lining their equipment needs.

**Grant recipients will be able to
use Artspace's Sony Hi8 and
audio equipment.**

Artists may request assistance with the full
project or only post-production needs.
*Non-residents of the greater Bay Area are
eligible for travel and per diem honoraria
up to $2,000.* Artists who have previ-
ously worked in mediums other than video
and feel that they have an idea that can best
be realized in video are encouraged to
apply.

C a t e g o r i e s   Experimental
Grants will be awarded
in the following genres   Narrative
including:
Editorial/non-fiction
Documentary

*The following is a list of equipment that
would every proposer will be*

Production
Sony Hi8 Video camera
Good collection of Mic's (Sennheiser, A.K.G)
Fostex 4 Track Portable Recorder

Post Production
Sony VO-9850 3/4" Deck
Sony EVO-9800 Hi8 Deck
Sony RM-450 Editor
Fostex Model 450 8 Track Mixer
Fostex Model 80 8 Track Recorder

Amiga 2000 HD
Software for Amiga
Live 2000
Digipaint III
Invision Plus
Provideo Post Character Generator
Disney Animation Studio

Coming Soon
A/B Rolling Capability
Video Toaster
Time Base Code
Vector Scope

This program is open
to all artists and
independent pro-
ducers who are not
students.
Grants will be
awarded to artists
living anywhere in
the world. Interna-
tional artists should
note that equipment
will be limited to
the San Francisco
Bay Area.
The video must be
non-commercial in
nature.

EliGiBiLiTy

application   *procedure*

1). Send a one-page project description, time length of proposed
completed video project, outline of equipment needs, project timeline,
and resume to: **San Francisco Artspace**
1286 Folsom Street
San Francisco, California 94103.

Also note source and amount of any other production monies which
have been awarded for proposed project
2). Semi-finalists will be asked to submit sample work
3). Applications will be reviewed three times a year. Applications
should be received at Artspace by 5:00 p.m. of the deadline date.

Selection ■ P R O C E S S

A jury of individuals working in different disciplines will review applications. Grants will be
awarded to original, thoughtful proposals.
Artspace will determine with the selected
artists a time period during 1991 to use the
equipment and facilities.

Completion *and* Presentation

• Artist will be required to complete their video projects within one year.
• The artist will be provided with two copies of the videotape.
• Artspace will host a public screening twice a year for all completed videos.
Artspace will have the right to premier videotapes. The artist will provide Artspace
with 2 copies
of the tape to be shown at our discretion for non-commercial use.
• The artist will include a credit to San Francisco Artspace in all screenings.

Liability and Rights

1.] Written material and related works will only be
viewed by the jurors and will not be made public.
2.] Sample works will only be returned if a self ad-
dressed stamped envelope is provided by artist.
3.] San Francisco Artspace will make every effort to
properly handle application and sample work, but is
not responsible for loss or damage to the works.
4.] All rights, excluding the right to screen the
videotape at Artspace, and ownership of the completed projects will belong to the artist.

Deadlines:
January 15, 1991
May 1, 1991
September 15, 1991

Grant Announcements:
February 28, 1991
June 30, 1991
October 31, 1991

415-626.9100
415-431.6612

San Francisco Artspace, *1286 Folsom Street,*
San Francisco, California 94103

International call for proposals. Poster. San Francisco Artspace, USA, 1990. Design John Weber

Poster/flyer. Columbus Society of Communicating Arts, USA, 1990. Design John Weber, Rudy VanderLans

TCR 01:0

Created designed edited keeper of the flame?

Non-Stop

design

circus

CSCA Guest Speaker

RUDY
VANDERLANS EMIGRE
(em'ə grā')

(non-stop design)

mag
azin
e

April
19
THURSDAY 6:30 Social hour
7:30 ANNOUNCEMENTS
7:45 presentation

AT
THE PHOTOGRAPHIC ILLUSTRATORS
GREEN MEADOWS CORPORATE PARK
404 ENTERPRISE DRIVE
WESTERVILLE

oh

PRINTERS AND

PUBLISHING

AND

typographic services

445 YORK STREET

type   samples

THE

COMPANY

TYPOC POCRAFT

313   832.   6700

DETROIT, MICHIGAN 48202

LITHOGRAPHERS

left: Type samples poster
The Typocraft Company, USA, 1990
Design Allen Hori

right: Advertisement
Gonzgraphics, USA, 1990
Design Barry Deck
Photography: Charles Field

Linotronic Imaging and Stat Center

GONZGRAPHIC

3325 West Wilshire Boulevard SUITE 305

LOS ANGELES
California
90010

Scanning

Linotronic L300

QMS COLORSCRIPT

LASERWRITER II NTX

FAX 12133851905
MODEM 12133857750

telephone
[213]385-4815

Design: Barry Deck
Photography: Charles Field
This page printed.
Yours will too.

GONZGRAPHICS

3325 Wilshire Boulevard
suite 305
Los Angeles
California
90010

Emily   Ginsberg   **Printmaking   Department**   Roger   Allen-Wickler
Miranda   Maher   **Cranbrook   Academy   of   Art**   Susan   Benarcik
Renee   Angele'   Mason   Anne   Cousino
Kathleen   McShane   Todd   Duren
Debra   Durst

ENGINES oF PERCEPTION

rrrrrrrrrrrrrrrr   aaahhhhhhhh

Lisa   Moren
Steve   Murakishi
Kreigh   Rasikas
Manual   Rodriguez
Slusser   Gallery/ School of Art/ University of Michigan
2000 Bonisteel Boulevard/ Ann Arbor, MI 48109
JULY 9 - AUGUST 10/ 1990   Shimmi   Sikand
Joe   Sim
Joann   Thornton
John   Tinnin

P. Scott Makela

Engines of perception. Exhibition invitation
Cranbrook Academy of Art, USA, 1990
Design P. Scott Makela

map *map* **Map**

𝔐𝔦𝔯𝔱𝔥

GLOW

sip GLASS   *giggle*

WINE   GLASS   FORK

FORK   Grilled Salmon

Bavette   SPOON
PLATE   PLATE

BREAD

FRIEND   NAPKIN   *Friend*

CHAIR   CHAIR

NAPKIN

loafers   *pump*s

CRUMBS

RESTAURANT
(FLORENT)
69 GANSEVOORT STREET
929-5779

Mirth. Postcard
Restaurant Florent, USA, 1989
Design Marlene McCarty, Tibor Kalman M&Co

above: *Vout:oroonie*
Club poster/flyer. UK, 1990
Design Designers Republic
opposite: *Fact Twenty Two*. Poster. USA, 1990. Design Rudy VanderLans, James Towning

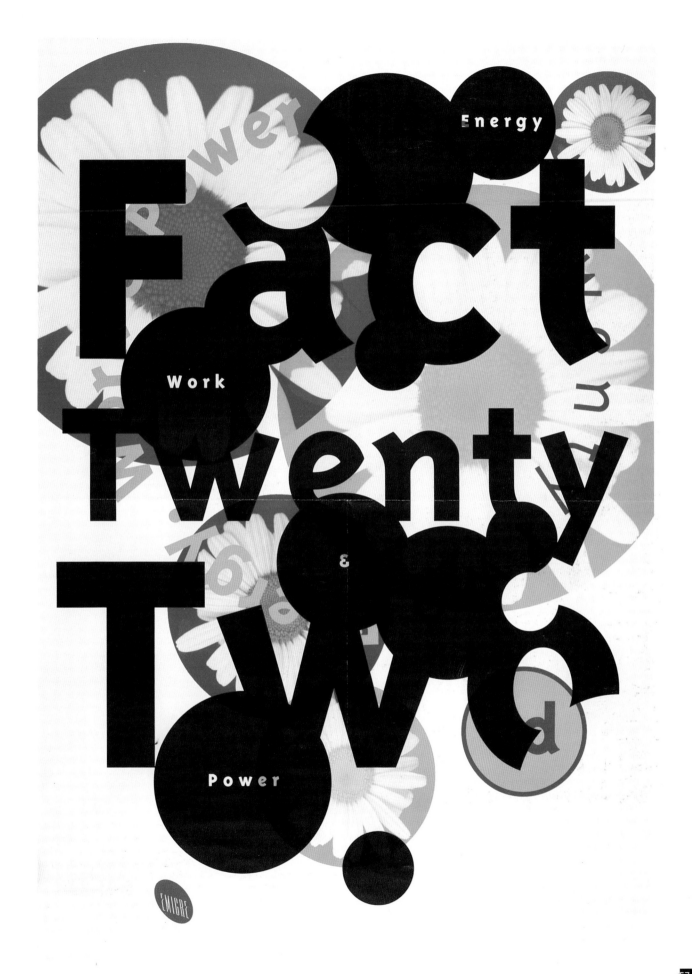

Fact Twenty Two

Energy

Work

&

Power

EMIGRE

Public Enemy's first record, *Yo! Bumrush the Show*, went gold. Their second record, *It Takes a Nation of Millions to Hold Us Back*, went platinum. The single "Fight the Power" (from their third and most recent album, *Fear of a Black Planet*) was the musical theme of Spike Lee's *Do the Right Thing*. *Fear of a Black Planet* went platinum in one week. These figures might not be so impressive if the act were a middle-of-the-road act, but Public Enemy pulls no punches, and there is no shortage of controversy over their lyrics. They have become cultural heroes, representing the truth of urban America in no uncertain terms: "Elvis was a hero to most/but he never meant shit to me you see/Straight up racist that sucker was/Simple and plain/Motherfuck him and John Wayne"— from the single "Fight the Power."

In early 1983 a mobile D.J. collective known as Spectrum City was roaming around Roosevelt, Long Island, playing hip-hop in the parks and broadcasting their highly influential Super Spectrum Mixx Show on the Long Island radio station WBAU on Saturday night. At the forefront of all the action was a powerhouse jester/M.C. named Flavor Flav, whose antics and energy brought him into local prominence. It was also in Spectrum City that **Flavor Flav** began his collaboration with producer Hank Shocklee and another resident of the 'Velt, named Chuck D. Chuck had studied the speech patterns of minister Louis Farrakhan, and by blending this dynamic oratory with a keen political consciousness and a Madison Avenue knack for phrase-mongering, Chuck established himself as one of the most powerful voices in rap. In 1986 Flavor Flav, Chuck D, and a D.J. named Terminator X formed Public Enemy. As his name suggests, Flavor Flav was the perfect counterpart to Chuck D's heavily important, hard-core approach to rap. Sometimes Flavor Flav adds spice, accent, or salt, but most often his voice is inserted as a kind of hydraulic adrenaline boost, loopy and cartoonlike against Chuck's straight-ahead drilling. A master at playing "the dozens" (a ritual requiring steady wit to out-insult your opponent), Flavor Flav can be as biting as he is hilarious. But as he proves on the record's hit single "911 is a Joke," when Flavor Flav takes over the role of lead rapper, he commands serious respect.

i'm black and i'm **proud** i'm ready and hyped plus i'm **amped** most of my heroes don't appear on no stamps **sample** a look back you look and find nothing but rednecks for 400 years if you check don't worry be happy was a **number** one jam...

above: *Interview*. Magazine pages
Brant Publications, USA, 1990

Creative director Tibor Kalman
Design Kristin Johnson
Photography: Josef Astor

athol fugard **gives** the impression that **doing** the **right** thing is **easy,** that doing **the** right thing **makes** you **feel alive,** that **it** is as **easy** as breathing to **know** the **right** way from **the wrong** way.

Interview. Magazine pages
Brant Publications, USA, 1990
Creative director Tibor Kalman
Design Kristin Johnson
Photography: David Lee

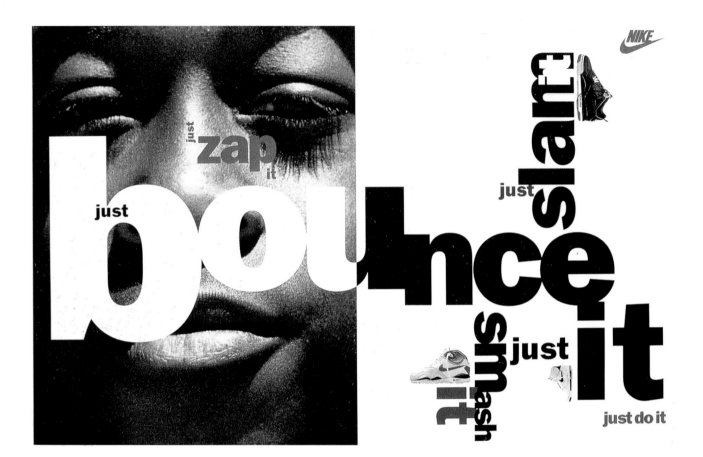

above: *Just slam it*
Advertising campaign. Nike, USA, 1989
Design Neville Brody
Agency: Wieden and Kennedy

Interview. Magazine pages
Brant Publications, USA, 1990
Creative director Fabien Baron
Photography:
Wayne Maser

IGGY

pop

rob lowe

left: *Interview*. Magazine pages
Brant Publications, USA, 1990
Creative director Fabien Baron
Photography: Albert Watson
below: *Per Lui*. Magazine pages
Condé Nast, Italy, 1990
Art director Neville Brody

fOrma

Definizione: «La forma è l'aspetto di un oggetto, sufficiente a caratterizzarlo esteriormente». Shape, in inglese. È la struttura, la linea, il risultato di una manipolazione, di una creazione: il frutto della natura, della mano dell'uomo. È la natura, è l'uomo. È ciò che sta fuori: il racconto visivo, la sintesi di quel che sta dentro. È il disegno, il pensiero che si può toccare, la certezza; la rassicurazione che quella cosa, quell'oggetto esistono davvero. Già, ma perché la forma? Perché tentare di rappresentare la nostra vita attraverso le forme? Perché forma è tutto, e tutto ha una forma. A partire dall'universo – un'immensa cupola? – e prima ancora dal «caos», come spiega il giornalista Peter Glaser, «la forma di tutte le forme, l'inizio della storia». Che oggi ritorna nei frattali, cioè le rappresentazioni grafiche di formule ▸

opposite: *Howl* by Allen Ginsberg (German translation)
Book pages. Germany, 1991
Design Lars Ohlerich
Hochschule für Gestaltung
Offenbach

below: *Howl* by Allen Ginsberg
Book pages. Germany, 1991
Design Peter Biler
Hochschule für Gestaltung,
Offenbach

above: *Dance for the new decade*
Margaret Jenkins Dance Company, USA, 1988
Design Tom Bonauro
Photography: Ken Probst

right: *Rearrange.* Greetings card
Pillow Talk Cards, USA, 1991
Design Tom Bonauro

Tocsin. Album cover. 4AD, UK, 1984. Design Vaughan Oliver
Photography: Nigel Grierson

Fetisch. Album cover (back)
4 A D, UK, 1983
Design Vaughan Oliver

above: *L'Esclave endormi.* 12" single (front and back). 4AD, UK, 1986
Design Vaughan Oliver
Photography: Nigel Grierson

left: *Le mystère des voix Bulgares*
Album cover. 4AD, UK, 1988
Design Vaughan Oliver
Photography: Simon Larbalestier

Doolittle. Album cover. 4AD, UK, 1989
Design Vaughan Oliver
Photography: Simon Larbalestier

Xymox. 12" single cover. 4AD, UK, 1987
Design Vaughan Oliver
Photography: Jim Friedman

Black Francis: Vocals, Guitar

Kim Deal: Bass, vocals

David Lovering: Drums, vocals

Joey Santiago: Lead Guitar

Robert F. Brunner: Theremin

Velouria

BAD 0009

1 **Velouria**

2 **Make Believe**

Produced by Gil Norton

3 **I've Been Waiting For You**

4 **The Thing**

Art Direction and Design: Vaughan Oliver / v23

Photography: Simon Larbalestier

Made in England

4AD

Velouria. 12" single cover (back). 4AD, UK, 1990. Design Vaughan Oliver Photography: Simon Larbalestier

right: Brochure. Seymour Powell. UK, 1989
Design Siobhan Keaney
Photography: Robert Shackleton

below: Price card. P.Inks LA. USA, 1989
Design Tom Bonauro

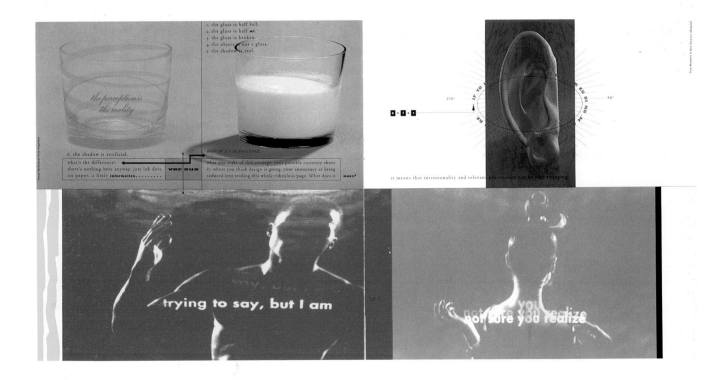

Enter. Call for entries

American Center for Design, USA, 1989

Design Rick Valicenti Thirst

OF THE NINETIES ▶▶ one of these seeds can grow up to be an apple.

1 can grow up to be an orange.

COMPEAR

SOWS

that what you think

you saw may not be

there's no physical resemblance between the seed and the fruit. the relationship is multi-dimensional. besides material and information, it needs time, nourishment, and a safe place 2 grow the just-born seed of a new idea doesn't look like much, either. but an apple changed the shape of the universe when it hit Newton's head. anything interesting hitting your head these days?

thread
spontaneity

intuitive

connection

discipline
fantasy

responsibility freedom

global local

black fascinating

TIME
WILL
TELL

5

Mildred Friedman
design curator walker art center minneapolis
Tibor Kalman
m & co. new york
Gert Dumbar
studio dumbar holland
Michael Mabry
michael mabry design san francisco
Eric Martin
consultant in information theatre los angeles

Rick Valicenti
1989 STA 100 SHOW chairperson

what I meant unless

2

you believe that I

so does resistance

In each case, in order to achieve this distinctive aesthetic quality we worked at the limits of the technology of the day. In some instances the frontiers were extended by some innovations. I have already mentioned the use of epoxy glued joints and pre-stressing on the Opera House, the essential role of computers, and developments in glass technology. There was also the development of non-ferrous metals for certain fixings (we even used titanium), as well as in the surveying techniques which were complex as a consequence of the geometry of the building. But above all, while the basic sculptural composition was an architectural or artistic concept, the subsequent geometric discipline to which we subjected the building resulted in a clear expression of the underlying engineering forms.

What I have spoken about is engineering in the service of architecture. It is an activity that can of course have its frustrations — I suppose all human endeavour has its trials as well as its tribulations. And in these days of specializations, it is more important than ever to concentrate on human qualities as much as on technical ones. However brilliant the engineer and architect, if they cannot or will not communicate or work together effectively, the building will suffer. We must learn to understand the problems of our collaborators and when we do and they understand ours, engineering is or should be a creative and challenging activity. And when it is associated with interesting, or even better, great architecture, it can be exciting and very rewarding."

Excerpt from a lecture given by Jack Zunz at the Royal College of Art, London, on December 17, 1987 in association with the College's 150th Anniversary "Great Engineers" Exhibition.

Ove Arup & Partners California

invites you to a reception in honor of Sir Jack Zunz

Sir Jack Zunz is an internationally recognized structural engineer. Recently retired as Chairman of the Ove Arup Partnership, he has collaborated with many prominent international architects on such significant buildings as the Sydney Opera House and the Hongkong and Shanghai Bank Headquarters. In 1980, he was awarded the Gold Medal of the Institution of Structural Engineers and in 1989 received Knight Bachelor for services to the profession by the Queen of England. In March of this year, he was made an Honorary Fellow of the Royal Institute of British Architects.

Sir Jack Zunz

Monday, October 29, 1990
5:30 pm to 8:00 pm

The Atrium
901 Market Street
San Francisco

RSVP by October 26
415 957 9445

An exhibit featuring the work of Ove Arup & Partners California will be on display in The Atrium Gallery, October 29 through December 7, courtesy of The Lurie Company.

On Tuesday, October 30, Sir Jack Zunz will speak on the Aesthetics of Technology at the twelfth annual lecture series on contemporary architecture sponsored by the San Francisco Museum of Modern Art and the San Francisco American Institute of Architects.

Michael Lewis, Ove Arup, and Jack Zunz at the Sydney Opera House site, 1966

architecture

integration

technology

engineering

opposite:
Sir Jack Zunz. Invitation
Ove Arup & Partners, USA, 1990

Workspirit. Magazine cover. Vitra,
Switzerland, 1988
Design April Greiman

Two Machines

Lifeguard Tower
County of Los Angeles, CA

The Flying Project
Mobile Dance Theater

Holt Hinshaw Pfau Jones now has a Los Angeles office, downtown just off the Santa Monica Freeway at 967 McGarry Street

Cold Water

UCLA Chiller Complex
The University of California at Los Angeles

everyday learning a process of discovery.
Marshall McLuhan

Holt Hinshaw Pfau Jones

Two Working Buildings

Paramount Pictures
Hollywood, CA
Film and Tape Archive and Editing Facility

Right Away Redy Mix
Oakland, CA

Architecture

the possibility of arranging the entire human environment
as a work of art, as a teaching machine

Holt Hins... Pfau Jones

Overlake Sector
Bridgeway Science and Industry Network, CA

e now become
aware of

Architects' brochure/poster
(front and back). Holt Hinshaw Pfau Jones, USA, 1989
Design 8vo

A National
Monument

Astronauts Memorial
Kennedy Space Center, Florida

Holt Hinshaw Pfau Jones

maximize perception and to make

making

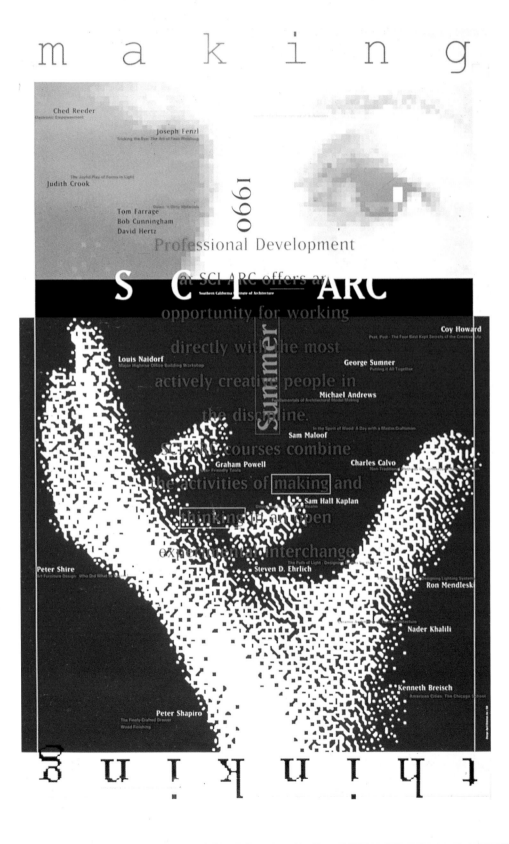

Ched Reeder
Electronic Empowerment

Joseph Fenzl
Tricking the Eye: The Art of Faux Finishing

The Joyful Play of Forms in Light
Judith Crook

Down 'n Dirty Materials
Tom Farrage
Bob Cunningham
David Hertz

1990

Professional Development

at SCI-ARC offers an

opportunity for working

directly with the most

actively creating people in

the discipline.

SCI-ARC courses combine

the activities of making and

thinking in an open

experimental interchange.

S C I ARC
Southern California Institute of Architecture

Coy Howard
Post, Post - The Four Best Kept Secrets of the Creative Life

Louis Naidorf
Major Highrise Office Building Workshop

George Sumner
Putting it All Together

Summer

Michael Andrews
Fundamentals of Architectural Model Making

In the Spirit of Wood: A Day with a Master Craftsman
Sam Maloof

Graham Powell
Friendly Tools

Charles Calvo
Non-Traditional

Sam Hall Kaplan

Steven D. Ehrlich

Ron Mendleski

The Path of Light - Designing

Peter Shire
Art Furniture Design: Who Did What to Whom

Nader Khalili

Kenneth Breisch
American Cities: The Chicago School

Peter Shapiro
The Finely-Crafted Drawer
Wood Finishing

thinking

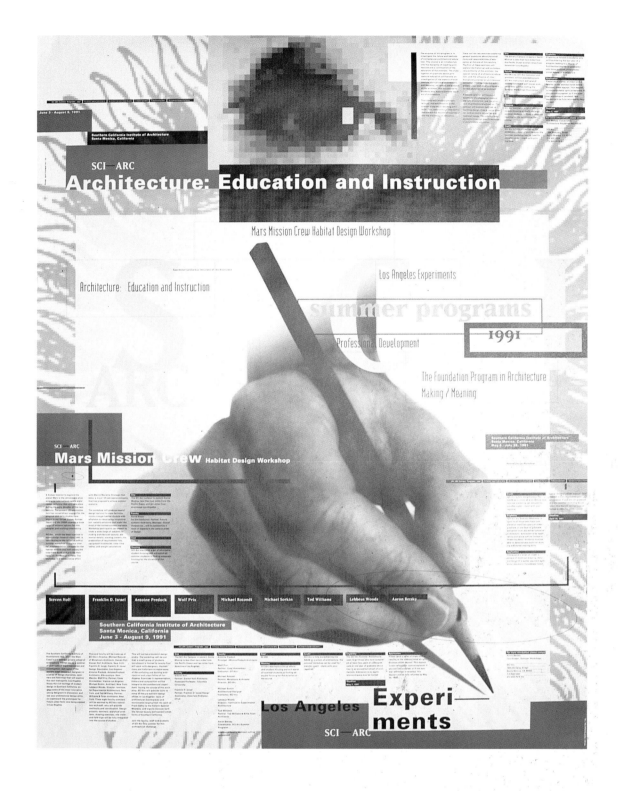

Sci Arc: summer programs. Poster
Southern California Institute of Architecture,
USA, 1991
opposite:
Sci Arc: making/thinking. Poster
Southern California Institute of Architecture,
USA, 1990
Design April Greiman

Eye: Communication Graphique

A Graphic Communication:

Grafische Kommunikation:

51.30ɴ 0.10ᴡ

opposite: *Eye magazine: a graphic communication*
Promotional poster. Wordsearch, UK, 1990
Design Cartlidge Levene
Photography: Richard J. Burbridge

Issue. Magazine pages
Design Museum, UK, 1991
Design Cartlidge Levene
Photography: Richard J. Burbridge

This is the night, **(hæc nox est),** when the pillar of fire destroyed the darkness of sin. This is the night, **(hæc nox est),** when Christians everywhere, washed clean of sin & freed from all defilement, are restored to peace & grow together in holiness. This is the night, **(hæc nox est),** when Jesus Christ broke the chains of death and rose triumphant from the grave.
MOST BLESSED OF ALL NIGHTS, **(O VERE BEATA NOX),** CHOSEN BY GOD TO SEE CHRIST RISING FROM THE DEAD.

Designed & printed by Phil Baines at the Royal College of Art, Easter 1987.

[o vere] **BEATA NOX:** MOST BLESSED OF ALL

NIGHTS, CHOSEN BY GOD TO SEE CHRIST RIS

ING FROM THE DEAD. [A candle for Easter 1988.]

Copyright Phil Baines, 1988. Published by Northern Heights.

[...]& vidit,& credidit: nonne vos: scio enebant Scriptudum enim scimm, quod Iesum, qui crucifiram, quia oporxus est, quær rtebat eum aitis: non est hic; mortuis

resurrexit
ri su esurre rgexit re.
tertia die, secundum Scripturas, [...]
en im, sicut dixit

The Creed   Jn. 20:8-9   Mtt. 28:5-6

Designed & printed by Phil Baines at Central Saint Martin's, March/April 1990, published by Northern Heights.

Paschal candles
Letterpress and silk screen
to fit 3' x 3" candle. UK, 1987-91
Design **Phil Baines**

A

This   This   This
is the night... is the night... is the night...

HÆC
NOX
EST

1 9
9 1

...when Jesus ...when Christ ...when first y
Christ broke t ians everywh ou saved our
he chains of d ere, washed c fathers; you f
eath & rose tr lean of sin & reed the peop
iumphant fro freed from all le of Israel fr
m the grave. om their slav
Des ery & led the
igned & prin m dry-shod t
ted by Phil Ba hrough the se
ines, iii 1991. a. *Exsultet*

defilement, an
e restored to
peace & grow
together in h
oliness.

u   a

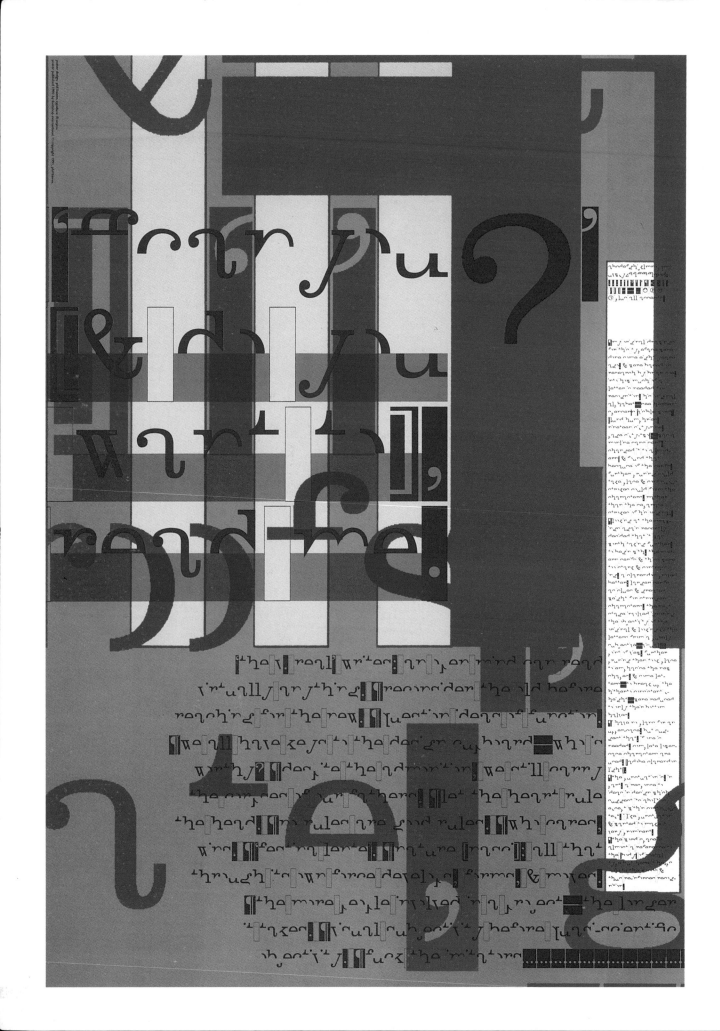

EX REJ
OIC hea
SUL nly po
wers, S
TET ING, c
hoirs of
iam A angels
.EXU
ngelic LT, al
l creat
a Jesu O
God's th
s CHR happy
rone
fault

CHR IST tu ,O necessary
sin of Adam,
which gained
IST yesterday and today, t OUR for us so great
he beginning and the end, KiNG rba a redeemer. Mos
t blessed of all nig
Alpha is RIS ris hts, chosen by Go
d to see CHRIST
and O EN. ing fro
Sound th
mega, e trum m the
al pet of salv
lt i ation .... dead.
m A cc
e belongs to him ep
, and all the age t this
s,TO HI EAsT
M B GL eR can
E dle, a fl
ORY and power thro ame di
ugh every age f vided,
or ever, AMEN. but undimmed, A PILLAR
OF FIRE that gro
ws to the glory of G O
od. Let it mingle w
ith the lights of hea
ven and c vere
ontinue b
ravely bu
rning TO
DIS beata
PEl
tHe
Dar
KNESS nox.
of this ni
ght. May
the morn
ing star which never sets fin
d this flame still burning: C
HRIST that morning star,
WHO CAME BACK FRO
M THe
DEAD. 1986
PhilBaine
s: March,

opposite: *F Can You . . . ?*
Poster for typographic magazine. *Fuse* issue 1, UK, 1991

Paschal candle
Letterpress to fit 3' x 3" candle. UK, 1986

Design Phil Bain
es

The t o

ce

pes
y

general brillian
of Baskerville's ty
was influenced b
the copybook desi
he himself was a
master. Thei
actual forms howe
relate far more c
to those found

gns: m

The english letter made its official a
ppearance in 1754 when the printer
, lettercutter, writing master and ja
panner *John Baskerville* began produ
cing his innovative letterforms: although t
here can be no doubt that his designs wer
e based on styles which had been develop
ed by tombstone carvers twenty or thirty
years previously. The clarendons, egyptian
s and **grotesques emerged from the
dense smoke of the Industrial Revo
lution round about 1800.** But long be
fore the first definitive forms appeared, m
any forms which now seem particularly E
nglish could be found in the primitive lett
erforms of early tombstones, builders' ma

b

writing

r

ver

rks and dates on houses, and even in Casl
on's types, derived though they were from
Dutch models.   Alan Bartram, quoted by Phil Baines

losely

on ········· stones.

With g
, stron
ed thi
on

Bound image. Page from an artists' book. Spacex Gallery, UK, 1988
Design Phil Baines

opposite:
Machine-generated stone-carving. UK, 1990
Design Jonathan Barnbrook

left: Promotional poster. Ora Lighting, UK, 1991
Design Russell Warren-Fisher

below: *Next Directory 7*. Section divider. Next, UK, 1991
opposite: *Next Directory 8*. Cover. Next, UK, 1991
Design Why Not Associates

BABYWEAR Next Babywear presents excellent design, colour and quality in the most innovative babywear collection available for 0 to 24 months. All accessorised with our colourful range of babies' footwear.
NEXT BOYS AND GIRLS Our Next Boys and Girls collection is the best-designed childrenswear available. Inspired by tropical summers, the range offers quality-conscious clothes that are practical, colourful and comfortable. All at affordable prices. For style conscious boys and girls from 2 to 8, our range is the tops.
NEXT BOYS AND GIRLS' ACCESSORIES A superb range of footwear and accessories. Uniquely designed for Boys and Girls aged 0 to 8, reflecting the style and design awareness of our clothing range.

244 babywear
NEXT BOYS AND GIRLS
250 next boys and girls
268 next boys and girls accessories

NEXT DIRECTORY

EIGHT 1991

NEXT 8
DIRECTORY

autumn winter EIGHT

NEXT **DIRECTORY**

№ 001133

DIRECTORY eIGHT

ladieswear collection
originals
eveningwear
lingerie
shoes and accessories

19 91

AUTUMN WINTER

93

Advertising campaign posters
Smirnoff vodka, UK, 1990
Design Why Not Associates
Photography: Why Not Associates,
Rocco Redondo
Agency: Young & Rubicam

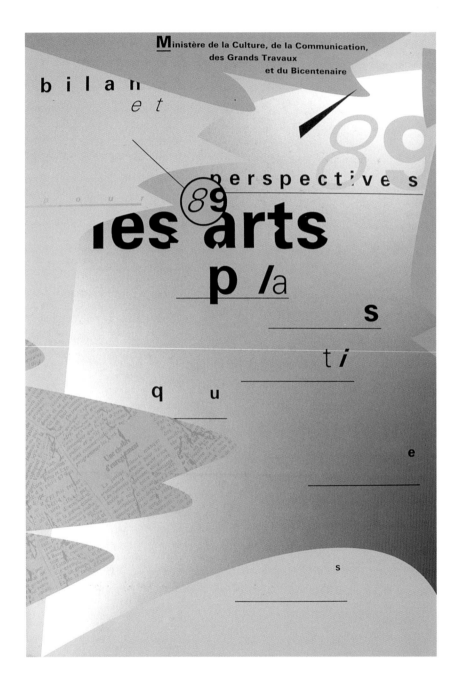

Les arts plastiques (The visual arts). Press kit cover. Ministry of Culture,
France, 1989. Design Philippe Apeloig

opposite:
Tabbles of Bower. Poster. Cranbrook Academy of Art, USA, 1991
Design Lisa Langhoff Vorhees

Jennifer Bloomer University of Florida College of
Architecture

Swanson Fund Lecture

10 December 1990 Monday 7:30 pm
CAA De Salle Auditorium

"TABBLES
O
F
BOWER"

Cranbrook Academy of Art Bloomfield Hills
Michigan

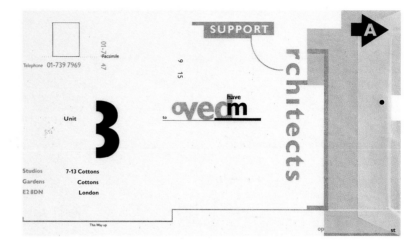

opposite:
Showreel labels. The Mill, UK, 1991
Design Siobhan Keaney

Moving card.
Support Architects, UK, 1989
Design Russell Warren-Fisher

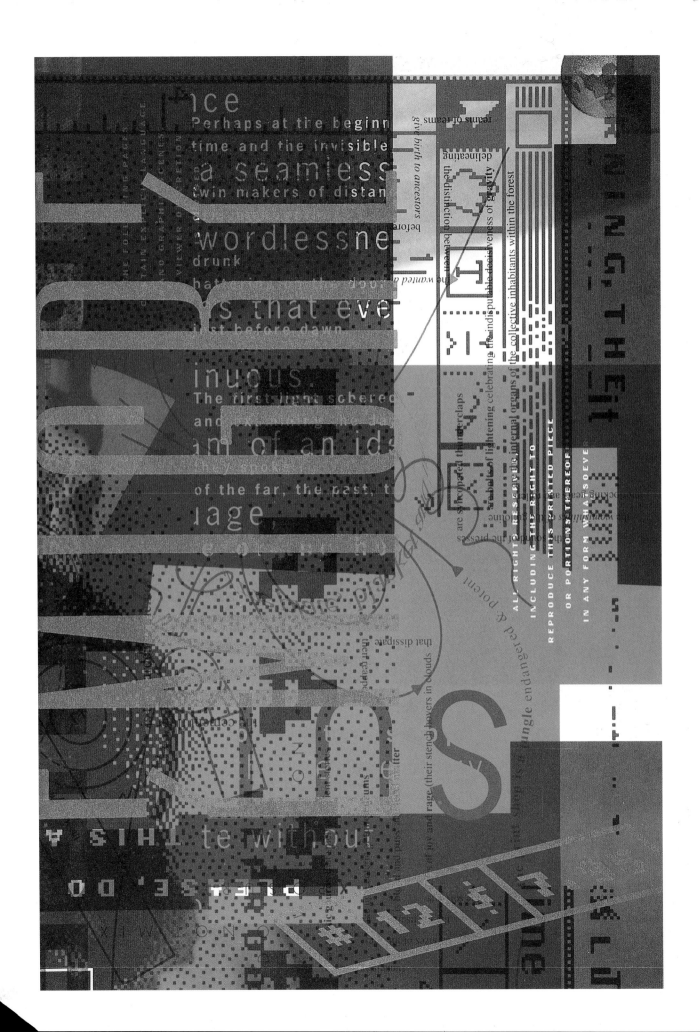

opposite page:

Emigre. Magazine cover. Emigre Graphics, USA, 1989

Design Allen Hori

Warren Lehrer

Phil Zimmerman

Rudy VanderLans

above:

Brody. Exhibition poster

Tempo magazine, Germany, 1989-90

left:

A. Type catalogue divider

FontShop, Germany, 1990

Design Neville Brody

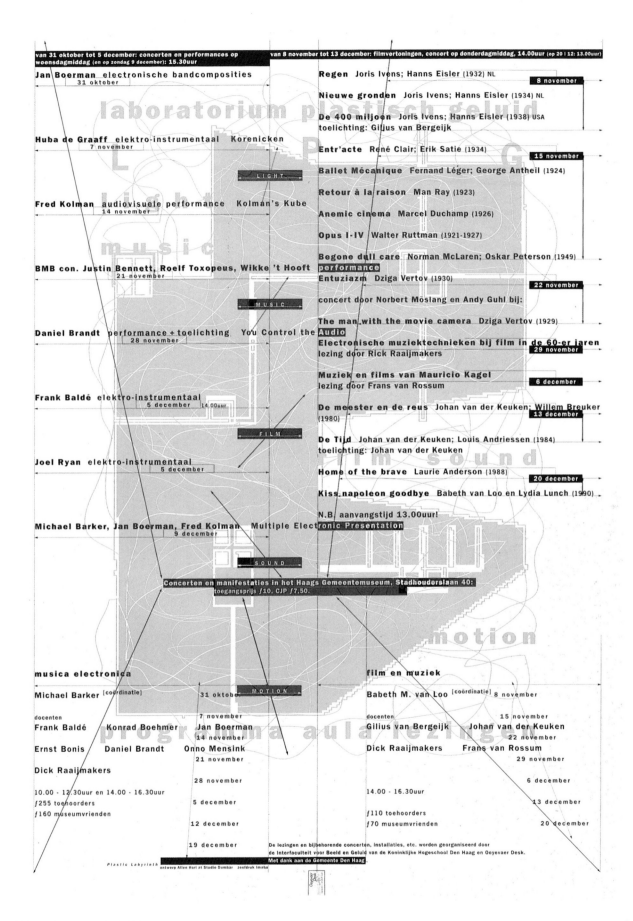

Laboratorium plastisch geluid (Laboratory of plastic sound). Poster
Ooyevaer Desk, The Netherlands, 1990. Design Allen Hori Studio Dumbar

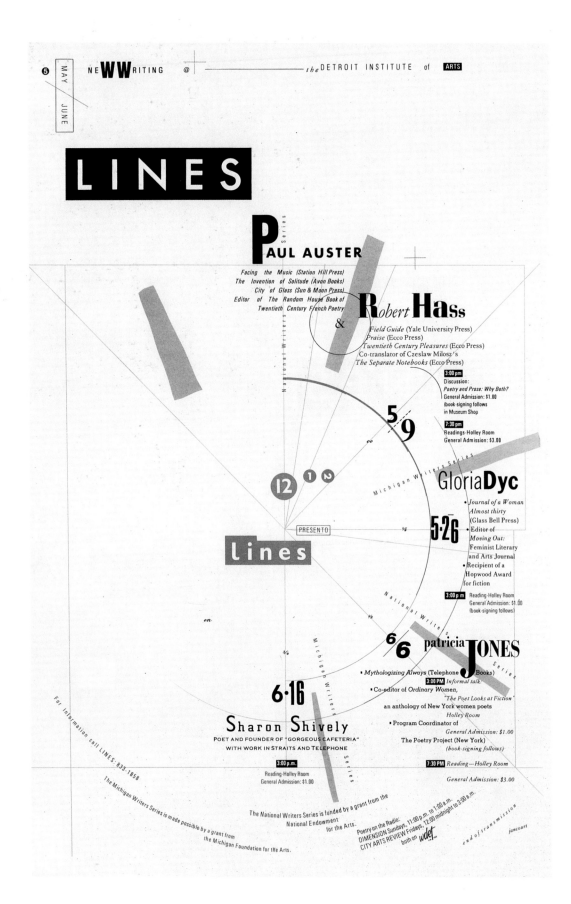

⑤ MAY / JUNE

NeWWRITING @ —————————— the DETROIT INSTITUTE of ARTS

LINES

PAUL AUSTER *Series*

Facing the Music (Station Hill Press)
The Invention of Solitude (Avon Books)
City of Glass (Sun & Moon Press)
Editor of The Random House Book of
Twentieth Century French Poetry

Robert **Hass**

Field Guide (Yale University Press)
Praise (Ecco Press)
Twentieth Century Pleasures (Ecco Press)
Co-translator of Czeslaw Milosz's
The Separate Notebooks (Ecco Press)

&

3:00 pm
Discussion:
Poetry and Prose: Why Both?
General Admission: $1.00
(book-signing follows
in Museum Shop

5 9

7:30 pm
Readings-Holley Room
General Admission: $3.00

National Writers Series

Michigan Writers Series

12 ① Ⓝ

Gloria**Dyc**

• *Journal of a Woman*
Almost thirty
(Glass Bell Press)

5·26

• Editor of
Moving Out:
Feminist Literary
and Arts Journal
• Recipient of a
Hopwood Award
for fiction

3:00 p.m Reading-Holley Room
General Admission: $1.00
(book-signing follows)

PRESENTO

Lines

National Writers

6 6 patricia **J**ONES *Series*

• *Mythologizing Always (Telephone* J *Books)*
3:00 PM *Informal talk:*
• Co-editor of *Ordinary Women,*
"The Poet Looks at Fiction"
an anthology of New York women poets
Holley Room
• Program Coordinator of
General Admission: $1.00
The Poetry Project (New York)
(book-signing follows)

7:30 PM *Reading—Holley Room*

General Admission: $3.00

6·16

S h a r o n S h i v e l y
POET AND FOUNDER OF "GORGEOUS CAFETERIA"
WITH WORK IN STRAITS AND TELEPHONE

Michigan Writers Series

3:00 p.m.
Reading-Holley Room
General Admission: $1.00

For information call LINES· 833-1858

The Michigan Writers Series is made possible by a grant from
the Michigan Foundation for the Arts.

The National Writers Series is funded by a grant from the
National Endowment
for the Arts.

Poetry on the Radio:
DIMENSION Sundays, 11:00 p.m. to 1:00 a.m.
CITY ARTS REVIEW Fridays, 12:00 midnight to 3:00 a.m.
both on wdet fm

end of transmission

jancourt

Contemporary improvised music festival. Poster. Ooyevaer Desk, The Netherlands, 1990
Design Allen Hori Studio Dumbar

opposite: *Lines.* Poster. Detroit Institute of Arts, USA, 1985. Design Jan Marcus Jancourt

The reading of gender. Poster. Detroit Institute of Arts, USA, 1989

opposite:

Typography as discourse. Poster. American Institute of Graphic Arts Detroit, USA, 1989

Design Allen Hori

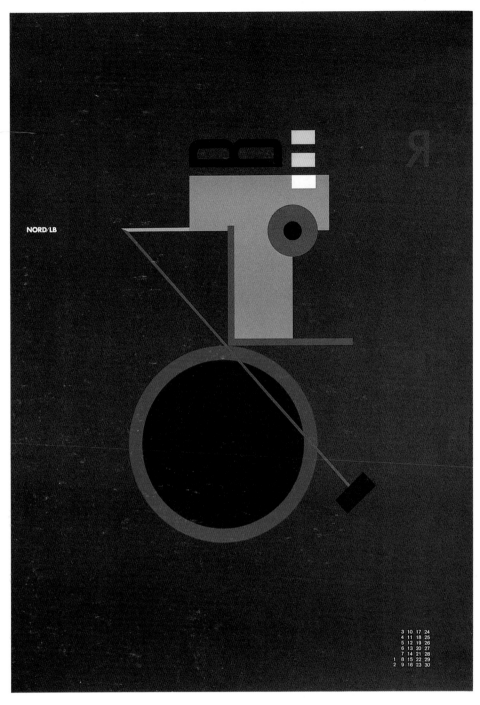

1991 calendar. Poster. Nord/LB,
Germany, 1990
Design Nicolaus Ott, Bernard Stein

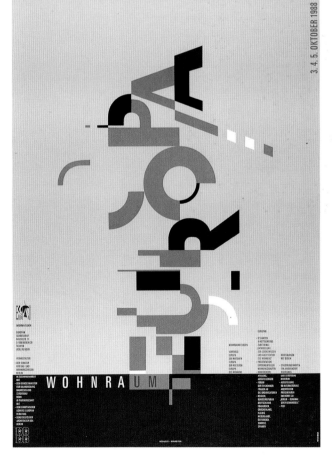

Beunos Aires. Symposium poster
Internationale Bauausstellung Berlin,
Germany, 1984
Design Nicolaus Ott, Bernard Stein

Wohnraum Europa. Poster
Berlin city council, Germany, 1988
Design Nicolaus Ott, Bernard Stein

i blow living the in a house down box

"blow the house down" by **living in a box.** available on 7", 12" and 7" limited edition package.

Chrysalis

opposite:

Living in a box. Poster
Chrysalis Records, UK, 1989
Design Why Not Associates

Tegentonen. Concert poster
Paradiso Amsterdam,
The Netherlands, 1987
Design Max Kisman

Diligentia seizoen 1988-89
(Diligentia season 1988-89)
Poster. Kunstring Dilgentia,
The Netherlands, 1988
Design Robert Nakata Studio Dumbar

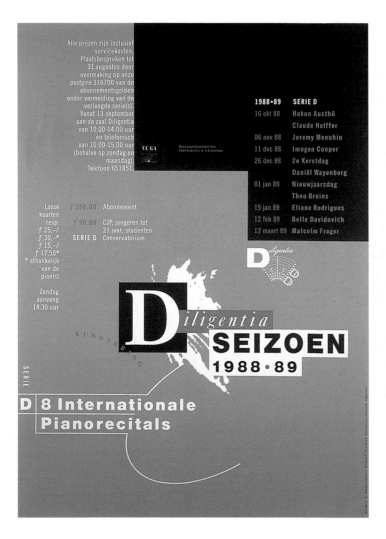

Haçienda seven. Club poster. Factory communications, UK, 1989. Design 8vo

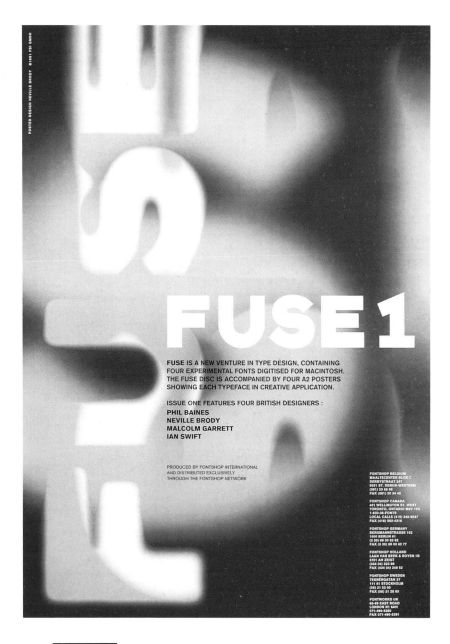

Fuse 1. Promotional poster. FontShop International, UK, 1991. Design Neville Brody

opposite:
Best wishes card.
Festival d'été de Seine-Maritime,
France, 1989
Design Philippe Apeloig

Poster / brochure
Jet Offset,
UK, 1991
Design 8vo

Haçienda Nine
21 May 1991
Fac 51

8vo

above:
Haçienda nine. Club poster
Factory Communications,
UK, 1991
Design 8vo

Jujol. Exhibition poster
Spain, 1990
Design Quim Nolla

opposite:
Tegentonen. Concert poster
Paradiso Amsterdam,
The Netherlands, 1991
Design Max Kisman

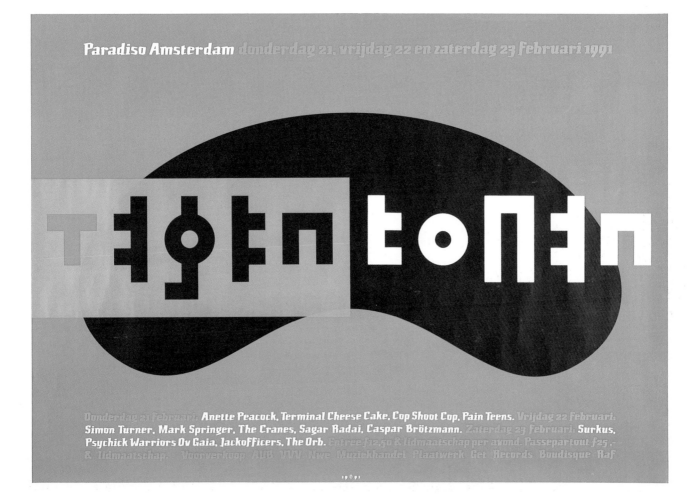

Paradiso Amsterdam donderdag 21, vrijdag 22 en zaterdag 23 Februari 1991

Donderdag 21 Februari: Anette Peacock, Terminal Cheese Cake, Cop Shoot Cop, Pain Teens. Vrijdag 22 Februari: Simon Turner, Mark Springer, The Cranes, Sagar Radai, Caspar Brötzmann. Zaterdag 23 Februari: Surkus, Psychick Warriors Ov Gaia, JackoFficers, The Orb. Entree f12,50 & lidmaatschap per avond. Passepartout f25,- & lidmaatschap. Voorverkoop AUB VVV Nwe Muziekhandel Plaatwerk Get Records Boudisque Raf

Vini Reilly-genius
  Poster
  Factory Communications,
  UK, 1990
Design 8vo

the durutti column

newalbumoutnow

...ly-genius...

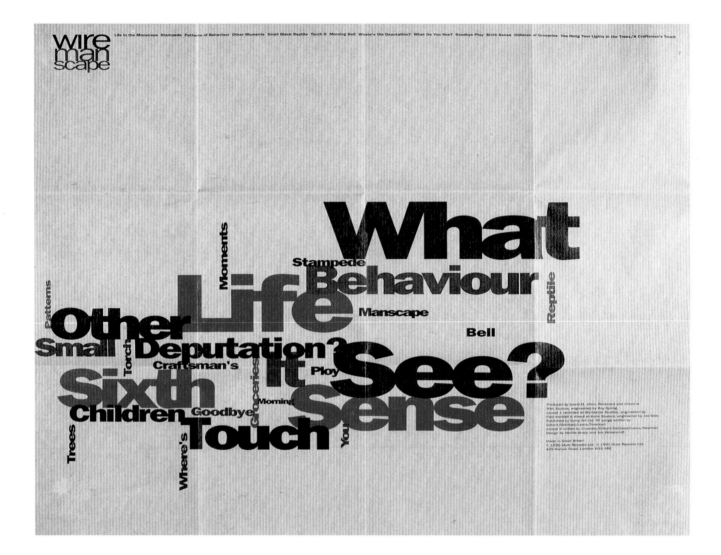

Life in the Manscape Stampede Patterns of Behaviour Other Moments Small Black Reptile Torch It Morning Bell Where's the Deputation? What Do You See? Goodbye Ploy Sixth Sense Children of Groceries You Hung Your Lights in the Trees/A Craftsman's Touch

Manscape. CD poster (back). Mute Records, UK, 1990
Design Neville Brody Jon Wozencroft

opposite:
Do you read me? Magazine cover. Emigre Graphics, USA, 1990
Design Rudy VanderLans

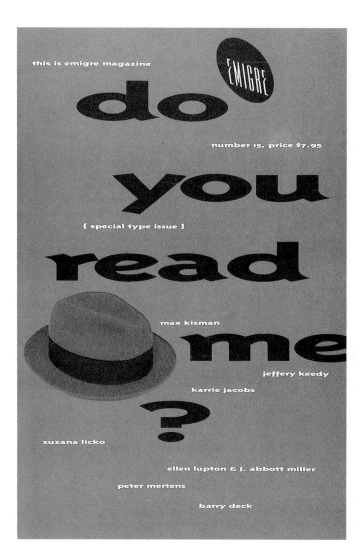

We're not printing a list of faces – it would take too much space and we've no doubt got what you want anyway. If you want to see them, just call for the books that not only give display and text samples for 1350 Berthold faces, but even contain useful information to enable the typographer to make considered judgements about exactly what to specify.

We have the latest Berthold equipment, the star in the typesetting firmament, and we're usually the first in the country to get the newest hardware and software. OK techno freaks, but what does that mean for the designer? Well, it means we're up to the minute technically but not to blind you with science, we understand the technics, you get the job you want – whether you like to be involved with the bits and bytes or just want the end result without knowing how we got there.

If you want to spec 10/11pt and leave the spacing up to us, that's fine, or you can spec everything in millimetres to the nearest 1/100mm and specify exact word and letter spacing to 192 unit increments. Either way, we understand what designers want. Our finely tuned aesthetics programme makes the most of any typeface – we really are talking accuracy and perfection.

We call ourselves Magic, because of the tricks we can do for you. We set type, rules, scan logos and artwork, and import images, all in position (forget your wax and scalpel).

int-lay, distor slant stretch,

Set complete documents in position with all the text linked to the pagination. Set packaging nets in position and save master nets so you can drop in new copy as required. And when you specify
then we output to film or bromide to a max image area of 300x760mm. Our film is good enough for the most exacting printer – no grey streaky blacks. And when you specify a 15% tint, that's exactly what you get – every time.

We also have the latest headline distortion equipment (more like a typo manipulation lab). If you thought the Mac was good for effects, wait until you see what this can do.

So what are we doing in darkest Macclesfield? Well actually, it's pretty nice here. And it means you won't be paying big city prices or dealing with big city egos. We are here to help you – we don't view our clients as an inconvenience. You can deal with people on the phone who understand your job, because they are the ones setting it! Not some remote telephone voice always looking for an excuse as to why it's late or too complicated to do. And we can get the stuff back to you fast – overnight by Datapost or courier, often same day by our own courier or Red Star (2 hours from Macclesfield to Euston). Most of our London clients proof-read laser outputs by fax first, so the bromides are right first time.
Magic Computer Graphics Co, Silk Mill, Thorp Street, Off Commercial Road, Macclesfield SK10 1LJ
Contact Granville Sellars
0625 612075

It really is magic. Promotional poster
Magic Computer Graphics Co, UK, 1990
Design 8vo

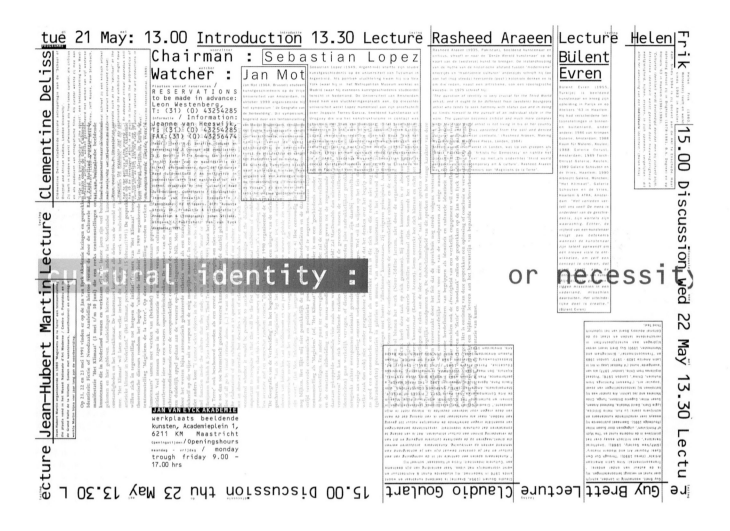

Cultural identity: or necessity. Symposium poster

Jan van Eyck Academy, The Netherlands, 1991

Design Ko Sliggers

Fractured Fairy Tales, Chaotic Regimes

Laura Trippi

> I had this phrase in my head,
> "What? Is this dancing?" "What is this? Dancing?"
> . . . . [T]he only thing left of *The Crucible* had to be the line
> "What is this dancing?" and there had to be a dance.
> —Elizabeth LeCompte

The ideas embedded in the language and images of "chaos science" strike a familiar, strangely seductive chord. Like the shapes and figures of its "fractal" geometry, our daily experience is fragmented; fraught with arbitrary juxtapositions, patterns of perception and social practice are assaulted by an onrush of information. "Reception," Walter Benjamin wrote as early as 1936, is "in a state of distraction, which is increasingly noticeable in all fields of art and is symptomatic of profound changes in apperception. . . ."[1] Faced with the demands of new computer and video technologies, we collectively confront a quantum leap in the state of distraction identified by Benjamin as a corollary of the emergence of film and photography. Leisure time, work, and art, our bodies and so also our selves — all are absorbed into the breathing and buzzing surreality of simulation culture, of global information networks and cybernetic machines.

"Chaos science" is an umbrella term for two related and emerging fields: fractal geometry and the study of complex dynamical systems. If its computer-generated video graphics strike in us a sympathetic chord — images of a randomized geometry and systems in chaotic states — perhaps it is because of our immersion in an atmosphere turbulent with new technologies. The guiding myths and models of modernity have been hopelessly infiltrated and frayed, and even the once invigorating concept of "crisis" itself seems to have collapsed. This is a journey into space — the "phase space" of turbulence and "sensitive dependence"; of "multidimensional degrees of freedom"; of the decay, creation, and random fluctuation of information. It began as an experiment, a gamble, an *essay* in the sense of an attempt or try, a search for the strangely fractured fairy tales of an emerging regime.

Border Regions

Benoit Mandelbrot's compendium and guidebook, *The Fractal Geometry of Nature*, was published in 1983. In 1985, Goethe House New York sponsored the first exhibition of fractal graphics, produced by scientists and offered in unaltered photo-reproductions as art.[2] By the mid-eighties, the shapes and formulas of fractal geometry had begun to appear in the work of practicing artists. But forces other than the discourse of science seem to have prepared the ground for the expropriation of its latest images and ideas.

The term "fractal," a variant of "fractional," points to the idea both of fragmentation and irregularity. An emerging branch of geometry, the study of fractals breaks with the Euclidean tradition of idealized forms. With an infinite nesting of pattern within pattern, repeating across scales, fractal images open onto an area devoid of fixed coordinates. Because the mathematical operations that produce fractal "landscapes" depend on the introduction of chance (random number generation), each repetition of a given pattern asserts a fractional difference from all others. The notion of boundary, too, is confounded. On closer look, the line dividing two regions reveals unexpected complexity. In the literature, this is sometimes expressed as the

Strange attractors: signs of chaos
Exhibition catalogue: cover and pages
The New Museum of Contemporary Art, USA, 1989
Design Marlene McCarty, Tibor Kalman M&Co

> JAMES WELLING. I was trying to work beyond visibility, with notions of sense, sensuality, that which is of the senses.... I was engaged with other topics of which legibility, or representation,

WERE YOU AFTER A TENSION
James Welling
BETWEEN
Interviewed by
LEGIBILITY AND ILLEGIBILITY
Laura Trippi
IN THESE PHOTOGRAPHS?

always plays a part: hallucinations, extreme mental states, the drawings of psychotics–castles of detail, sensual, non-quotidian, non-representational. There were ideas about the wild, wilderness, nature, geological formations. Fabulous landscapes. Creating things that involve aspects of fiction or science fiction.

When I was working on the Aluminum Foil photographs, I understood that I was creating a program or a machine to

> LAURA TRIPPI. I just read a brief essay David Joselit wrote for your show in Vienna, which discusses your recent photographs of buildings by the late 19th-century architect H.H. Richardson. Joselit cites Richardson's aim as that of "disciplining the picturesque." The phrase caught my attention in connection with your Aluminum Foil photographs and the way they sort of traffic in the picturesque or sublime.

manufacture randomness, a system to make random images. It seemed extremely simple, straightforward, and *economical*, and also yielded all these images. This one piece of metal could be constantly refolded into itself. It was both a physical way to make pictures, and an analogy for other things, like language: the way language uses the same words but is constantly repermuted and reconfigured. The

> JW. I don't think we have feelings of the sublime anymore. It's a historical idea. I think these photographs do evoke a *lost* feeling of the sublime. The sublime I'm interested in is not a landscape, but more like snow on a T.V. screen. It has its own kind of beauty–if you can apply the word "beauty" to it. We're putting 19th-

century terms with a mid-20th-century electronic landscape.... But the idea of electronic snow, of raw electronic states, it was a pretty powerful idea. I don't think I've ever really talked about coming out of making video tapes and going into photography. But that was one of the reasons that, when I figured out what I wanted to do with the photograph, I worked the way I worked in the video studio, on a table top, with a tripod, etc.

986-7, James [Wel]ling produced a [ser]ies of "circle [pa]intings" that [app]ear a striking [r]esemblance to the "sphere [ex]tremas" of Mandelbrot, among the least obviously "fractional" of fractal images, printed in black-and-white in the book (*The Fractal Geometry of Nature*). In Welling's paintings, the massing shapes come across at once as vaguely ominous and profoundly pop, suggestive in this context of a deadpan commentary on the "promiscuity" of fractal graphics (even, more generally, on that [o]f simulation), the [sh]eer contagion of [the]ir allure.

The telephone book
Title page and book pages
University of Nebraska Press,
USA, 1989
Design Richard Eckersley

between two rooms, Bell's voice was vibrating from it, shouting "Ahoy! Ahoy!" "Are you there?" "Do you hear me?" "what's the matter?" ... Then began the first "long distance" telephone conversation the world has ever known. We recorded it word for word. The cavaliers made us do that. The common attitude toward any new thing is apt to be pessimistic for the average man thinks that what hasn't been done, can't be done. It was so with the telephone. It seemed a toy to most persons. Some of Bell's friends, although they had heard the thing talk in the laboratory were doubtful as to its practical value, and one of them of a scientific turn of mind told me that he didn't see how the telephone could be accurate enough for practical use for every spoken word has many delicate vibrations to be converted into electrical waves by the telephone and if some of these get lost the message cannot be intelligible. (A, 94–95).

The first long-distance electric conversation enveloped language in high-decibel noise; a certain kind of aberrancy. Ever since Watson had known Bell, his habit of celebrating successful experiments by what he called a war dance was respected, and "I had got so expert at it that I could do it as well as he could. That night, when he got back to the laboratory, we forgot there were other people in the house and had a rejoicing that nearly resulted in a catastrophe" (A, 95–96).

The morning after: "after a sleepless night, as I started down the stairs to go to Williams' to build some more telephones, I saw our landlady waiting for me at her door with an acid expression on her face" (A, 96). The waiting woman at the end of the line, steeped in the liquefying anger of experimental elements, her acid face about to have words. The naughty young man: "My conscience was troubling me and I felt something disagreeable was about to happen. My pretense of great haste did not work for she stopped me and said in an unpleasant voice, 'I don't know what you fellows are doing up in the attic but if you don't stop making so much noise nights and keeping my lodgers awake, you'll have to quit them rooms.' I couldn't say much to calm her. I assured her we would be more careful although for the life of me I didn't see how we could get along with any less noise than we had been making. I couldn't blame her

finding fault. She wasn't at all scientific in her tastes and we were not prompt with our rent" (A, 96). This is the only time Watson invokes the prerogatives of scientific sensibility, in the key of aesthetic taste, and we would not be wrong to suggest that he spits out the signifier with irony. The noise without which they would not be able to get along presumably resulted from the war dancing, as telephone connections were tried out in other spaces. Yet the inevitability—at however long a distance—of noise as a by-product of this innovation in the speech conveyance has just been announced to the landlady, whose figure is firmly planted to the ground. This may be the birth of

a new noise era

whose contours make Kafka's thin text,

"The Neighbor,"

explode.

The telephone was hardly a beloved or universally celebrated little monster. It inspired fear, playing on fresh forms of anxiety which were to be part of a new package deal of the invisible. This hardly replicates the way Watson puts it, yet he gives abundantly profiled clues to follow. It soon becomes clear that schizophrenia recognizes the telephone as its own, appropriating it as a microphone for the singular emission of its pain. Schizophrenia was magnetized by the telephone the way neurosis rapped on Freud's door. In a fundamental sense, we can say that the first outside call the telephone makes is to schizophrenia—a condition never wholly disconnected from the ever-doubling thing. Watson mounts his case slowly, describing the call of aberrancy first in terms of "embarrassment." Men in particular were uneasy about the thing. For instance: "It also interested me to see how many people were embarrassed when they used the telephone for the first time. One day a prominent lawyer tried the instruments with me. When he heard my voice in the telephone making some simple remark he could only answer after a long embarrassed pause, 'Rig a jig, and away we go'" (A, 98). Regression takes hold, the call transfers the speaker to a partial object, a false self caught up in the entanglement of fort/da: away we go.

Watson defines essentially two kinds of men that visited the telephone. The first we have just listened to, away he went. The second returns us to a recurrent concern, the consummate knowledge of disconnection that connects the schizophrenic to things and machinery: "Men of quite another stamp from those I have mentioned occasionally" (A, 98). Though he is not necessarily

The BAUHAUS mistook legibility for communication, (it's a man's world).

Nicolette Gray: in 1 p.12
'It is not really necessary for the beholder to read, or understand these words. THE WORDS ARE PART OF THE MEDIUM; what the artist is communicating through the medium is his reaction to, his understanding of these words, which he has expressed in the way they are inscribed.'

Six sheets, as if fragments, (keys to a larger argument/point of view: wider terms of reference lead to a better, more fully human typography), in order:-

1,2,3,4:

LEFT   RIGHT

FORGET   REMEMBER

SIGHT   SOUND

PRINT   MANUSCRIPT

INTO THE HOT...

'The system was basically very simple. The stationer held **a copy of the book** (exemplar) **unbound in** quires o**r pieces** (peci e), and hired i t out to a scri be piece by pi ece to copy.'

Richard Hunt: in 2 p. 202

James Sutton and Alan Bartram: in 3 p.26

'The Aldine Roman is the archetype of all Old Face types which during the sixteenth century established their ascendancy over gothic throughout Europe.'

'Grotesques, which **are closer** in some ways **to the black letter than the normal roman.'**

John Lewis: in 4 p.46

The Bauhaus mistook legibility for communication. Cover and page from college thesis, UK, 1985
Design Phil Baines

INTO THE HOT…

Ludwig Grote: i n 9 p.18

'PROPORTION WAS TO TAKE THE PLACE OF
SYNTHESIS TO REPLACE.
LOGICAL CONSTRUCTION
MECHANICS
COLLECTIVISM
SUCH WERE THE DEMANDS OF DE STIJL.'

Herbert B. Oliver : in 29

'The old ind ustrialism was unconcern ed with soul or spirit: it produc ed but for mon ey, colourless g oods that echo ed the charact eristics of any nation but our own. We cease ed to be. The s hekels buried u s. Our faith is g one in all that & we are like a sk eleton leaf-plan ts pressed in a b ook.'

Ivan Illic h: in 21 p. 13

'Institutions create certainties, and taken seriously, certainties deaden the heart and shackle the imagination.'

hy twice the n umber of sym bols, if half th e number acco mplishes the s ame thing?'

ver; discredited. **Broader terms of reference offer more possi bilities for finding a rich chaos** , subtle differences, (unity in vari ety), **an appeal to more of our b** eing and an affirmation of our tr ue potential and wealth. **Broade r terms of reference as somet hing to work from,** whatever th e goal- legibility, clarity or a rich, l ayered variety- **give typograph y its real kick,** its real utility or it s real wonder, and **it was broad er terms of reference that BA UHAUS codification stifled.**

BAUHAUS typography came t o assume as many gratuitous aesthetics as the work it reacted against, and the original aims we re soon lost. **Bauhaus disciples ignored many of the questio ns posed, scraped at, or ans wered on these six sheets; the y lacked** the **real pioneer spirit and zest** of El-Lissitsky, Alexand er Rodchenko, Kurt Schwitters or Piet Zwart; **the cheek** of Dada; **t he heat** of Hendrik Werkma n; the **rational historic ism** of Eric Gill **and** the **grace** of A nthony Fr oshau g.

FORM
. . ANALYSIS
. LYRICAL SUSPENSION
. CRAFTSMANSHIP
. INDIVIDUALISM

Mark E. Smith: o n 28

'All fashion i s filched off f aggots- then, two or more y ears later...'

In 30

'**R**ational , objectiv e thinking ca n produce be autiful art, b oth fine and a pplied. **What I find depres sing is the ex tent to whic h this approa ch is misappl ied.** In my vie w the best gr aphic design comes from p eople trained in other areas - notably pain ting and print making.'

overleaf: lan/gua/geb/rea/ksh/ere. Contribution to *Breakthrough* catalogue. Royal College of Art, UK, 1988. Design Phil Baines

lan gua ge|b

SA
"Bridal Bits"
salt **sel** **salz**

A dream come true
for 50p
wet & dry
whole cold
wet & wavy

50

(weave

18 x 12 x 18

(we

T H O N

-on)

19 x 21 x

Ste
Star

Terry's

s p e c i a l f i l t r e

◇◇◇◇◇◇◇◇◇◇◇◇◇◇

sta - sof - fro
ultra sheen afro
sheen
Fantasyclub

T **HE**
P **ANTRY**
    PEN

:

:

(weave -on)

• • • • • • •

D Share
jucy
mini

16 Ears p ierced
& 12 tun es

4 1 1 8 **bankrup t**

s   *e l*   *e c*   *t*

Mr. Juicy (**Steve.** Hu bba Bubb

words: david blamey. design: phil baines.

rea ks|h ere

Fresh

ave- on)

the critic

ice

's cho

V~T~ Ne ck

super

Big

gulf

(T
D)

op
eck

Va-Boy
90p. a pot

......&

wise
182
Yes,
we do!

"99"

knives

e   *d*

Lo		Sunny shoes
M	▦	wide approx
T	☐	any case
P	▦	Gary angels
E	▦	Sir sir sir
ut		No eels today

[s

a. Elvis Pr esley; Sam Fox; **Jesu**

publisher: billionth press, 1988. edition, 2000

Is there really a If there is, it coul d be just a fashion swing. After a sea son of th romantic brushstrokes a nd crayon effects, some e ar thin g more high-tech m rang ay b e in the air: a multi-l eme ayere d look of hard type on (. nt o ....) vi new enthusiasm fo r typography amo ng designers? ? deo textures. But what exactly is typography? f co mpo sed t ype.

Object quality: a quality which offered pleasure before, durin g and in excess of the pleasure of the content. If pressed I'd ha ve called it aesthetic pleasure, or more simply, the pleasure g

o the page, a well-ordered seq uence of pages, the quality of p restwork and binding. These a

iven to well made things. (...) Art appeal to the senses of sight and touch, the placing of type o

re traditional virtues. There a re others. (...) Searching for o bject quality is one of the most distinguishing features of typo

maniac. The tell-tale sympto ms are easy to spot: typomania
ca inspect, peer, hold, interro gate, discover: ....

Graphics World. Magazine cover illustration. Graphics World Publications, UK, 1989. Design **Phil Baines**

CalArts offers BFA and MFA degrees in each of its five schools;
Art, Dance, Film & Video, Music, Theatre.

The program in Visual Communication is one of the three programs – Art, Photography, and Visual Communication – that make up the School of Art. In keeping with the interdisciplinary emphasis at CalArts, students in the program in Visual Communication are strongly encouraged to make use of the resources and faculty of the other programs.

Catherine Lord
Dean, School of Art

California Institute of the Arts

Visual Communication

For almost two decades CalArts has encouraged a conceptual approach to the study of design, recognizing the necessity for professional competence without being limited by it.

AT A TIME WHEN BOTH CULTURAL CONTEXT AND TECHNOLOGICAL POTENTIAL ARE RAPIDLY CHANGING THE FIELD OF DESIGN, THE GRADUATE PROGRAM IN Visual Communication continues its commitment to an advanced exploration of practice and theory.

Graphic designers create much of our visual environment – in posters, signs, publications, advertising, packaging, information design, exhibitions, identity systems, computer graphics, and various electronic media. In preparation for the wide range of options within current design practice, the undergraduate program in Visual Communication at the California Institute of the Arts offers training in both practical and conceptual skills.

The first two years of study concentrate on basic design skills supplemented by classes in typography, photography, and drawing. Students are exposed to a purposeful variety of design methods, techniques, and philosophies to provide an understanding of complexity and technological change in the field. Because design is, first and foremost, about ideas, the program's core is a sequence of studio courses focusing on problem-solving and the cultural significance of design.

Guided by a faculty with an international reputation in graphic design, imagemaking, and information technology, each student develops an individual program of study by adding to the core sequence a combination of elective courses and independent study projects. The continuing definition of design goals and skills is aided by annual reviews of student work and the opportunity for students to work closely with a faculty advisor. By graduation students are expected to have produced a significant amount of work in print through participation in various graphic workshops. CalArt's proximity to the large and vital design community of Los Angeles provides ample opportunity for additional experience through part-time internships.

The graduate program in Visual Communication is demanding. A limited number of students are accepted in order to create a working community of designers, collaborating under the guidance of a faculty chosen for their professional expertise *and* their involvement in design research.

In studios, seminars, and independent study projects, issues of **critical theory, history, and design methodology** inform the development of a personal direction within the public context of **VISUAL COMMUNICATION**.

The program is pluralistic in scope, but not philosophy; the range of problems systematically posed reflects the conviction that a designer must transcend the conceptual limitations of much current professional practice in order to produce work that is once meaningful and original.

Assuming a high capacity for self-directed work, the community of designers in the graduate program in Visual Communication represents a deliberate mix of aesthetic and intellectual backgrounds. Those lacking specific skills are expected to require them in the first semester.

Independent work with an individual advisor, as well as semester reviews by the faculty, guide the student through the program.

Successful completion of an MFA degree requires the production of a coherent body of work, active participation in the community of designers, and the execution of an independent thesis project.

Financial aid and teaching assistantships are available.

Visiting Artists
Sue Coe
John Coy
James Cross
Henk Elenga
April Greiman
Mick Haggerty
Warren Lehrer
Michael Manwaring
Joe Molloy
Deborah Sussman
Lucile Tenazas
John Van Hamersveld
Rik Vermeulen
Phil Zimmerman

Faculty, Program in Visual Communication
Lorraine Wild, Director
Nancy Barton
Renee Cossutta
Dorothy Danziger
Lou Danziger
Dan Freeman
Louise Goodman
Jeffery Keedy
Eric Martin
Ann Phibbs
Nick Taggart

Faculty, Program in Visual Communication

Facilities
A well-equipped graphics lab for lithography, etching, silkscreen, letterpress, offset printing, and process camera work; typographic facilities ranging from a foundry press to a Mergenthaler ViP; Macintosh computer graphics facilities, with Laserwriter and digitizing equipment; color and mural darkrooms 20 x 24-inch color processor; color video studio, including two BY 110 cameras and on SEG, and a ¾-inch Sony S850 editing system with sound recording and mixing capabilities; five galleries for student exhibitions; periodic opportunities to create interdisciplinary work using institute resources, such as electronic music studios, 16-mm film facilities, and CMX editing.

Office of Admissions
California Institute of the Arts
24700 McBean Parkway, Valencia, CA 91355
or call 1-800-292-ARTS (California)
1-800-545-ARTS (out of state)

Visual communication. Faculty poster
California Institute of the Arts, USA, 1986
Design Jeffery Keedy, Lorraine Wild.

ID "Graphic design" issue. Magazine pages
Design Publications, USA, 1988
Design **David Frej**

Holland · Windmill Island · Wooden Shoe Factory · Dutch Village · Tulip Time · WOODEN SHOE FACTORY · Michigan

a so predisposed tourist has expectations based more or less on precise stereotypes.

The only dimension of time lying peacefully is hind us in the past,

While folk art grew from below, mass culture is imposed from above.

Emigre. Magazine pages
Emigre Graphics, USA, 1988
Design Lisa Anderson
Cranbrook Academy of Art

KATHERINE mcCoy
MICHAEL mcCoy

Art **science**

Nothing pulls you into the territory between art and science quite so quickly as design. It is the borderline where contradictions and tensions exist between the quantifiable and the poetic. It is the field between desire and necessity. Designers thrive in those conditions, moving between land and water. A typical critique at Cranbrook can easily move in a matter of minutes between

Mathematic **poetic**

a discussion of the object as a validation of being to the precise mechanical proposal for actuating the object. The discussion moves from Heidegger to the "strange material of the week" or from Lyotard to printing technologies without missing a beat. The free flow of ideas, and the leaps from the technical to the mythical. stem from the attempt to maintain a studio plat- form that supports each student's search to

Desire **necessity**

find his or her own voice as a designer. The studio is a hothouse that enables students

the and faculty to encounter their own visions of the world and act on them — a

new process that is at times chaotic, conflicting, and occasionally inspiring.

Watching the process of students absorbing new ideas and in- fluences, and the incredible range of in- terpretations of those ideas into design, is

Mythology **technology**

an annual experience that is always amaz- ing. In recent years, for example, the de-

discourse partment has had the experience of watching wood craftsmen metamorphose into high technologists, and graphic designers into software humanists. Yet it all seems consistent. They are bringing a very per- sonal vision to an area that desperately needs it. The messiness of human experi-

Purist **pluralist**

ence is warming up the cold precision of technology to make it livable, and lived in.

Unlike the Bauhaus, Cranbrook never embraced a singular teaching method or philosophy, other than Saarinen's exhortation to each student to find his or her own way, in the company of other artists and designers who were en- gaged in the same search. The energy at Cranbrook seems to come from the fact of

Individual **communal**

the mutual search, although not the mutual conclusion. If design is about life, why shouldn't it have all the complexity, vari- ety, contradiction, and sublimity of life?

Much of the work done at Cranbrook has been dedicated to changing the status quo. It is polemical, calculated to ruffle designers' feathers. And

Dangerous **rigorous**

Cranbrook design: the new discourse
Book page. Rizzoli, USA, 1990
Design Katherine McCoy
P. Scott Makela, Mary Lou Kroh

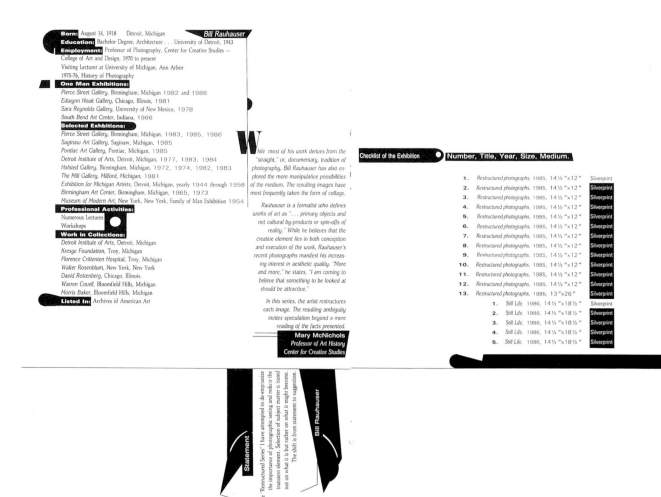

Born: August 14, 1918   Detroit, Michigan   *Bill Rauhauser*

Education: Bachelor Degree, Architecture . . . University of Detroit, 1943

Employment: Professor of Photography, Center for Creative Studies —
College of Art and Design, 1970 to present
Visiting Lecturer at University of Michigan, Ann Arbor
1975-76, History of Photography

One Man Exhibitions:
Pierce Street Gallery, Birmingham, Michigan 1982 and 1986
Edwynn Houk Gallery, Chicago, Illinois, 1981
Sara Reynolds Gallery, University of New Mexico, 1978
South Bend Art Center, Indiana, 1966

Selected Exhbitions:
Pierce Street Gallery, Birmingham, Michigan, 1983, 1985, 1986
Saginaw Art Gallery, Saginaw, Michigan, 1985
Pontiac Art Gallery, Pontiac, Michigan, 1985
Detroit Institute of Arts, Detroit, Michigan, 1977, 1983, 1984
Halsted Gallery, Birmingham, Michigan, 1972, 1974, 1982, 1983
The Mill Gallery, Milford, Michigan, 1981
Exhibition for Michigan Artists, Detroit, Michigan, yearly 1944 through 1958
Birmingham Art Center, Birmingham, Michigan, 1965, 1973
Museum of Modern Art, New York, New York, Family of Man Exhibition 1954

Professional Activities:
Numerous Lectures
Workshops

Work in Collections:
Detroit Institute of Arts, Detroit, Michigan
Kresge Foundation, Troy, Michigan
Florence Crittenten Hospital, Troy, Michigan
Walter Rosenblum, New York, New York
David Rottenberg, Chicago, Illinois.
Warren Covell, Bloomfield Hills, Michigan
Morris Baker, Bloomfield Hills, Michigan

Listed In: Archives of American Art

While most of his work derives from the "straight," or, documentary, tradition of photography, Bill Rauhauser has also explored the more manipulative possibilities of the medium. The resulting images have most frequently taken the form of collage.

Rauhauser is a formalist who defines works of art as ". . . primary objects and not cultural by-products or spin-offs of reality." While he believes that the creative element lies in both conception and execution of the work, Rauhauser's recent photographs manifest his increasing interest in aesthetic quality. "More and more," he states, "I am coming to believe that something to be looked at should be attractive."

In this series, the artist restructures each image. The resulting ambiguity invites speculation beyond a mere reading of the facts presented.

Mary McNichols
Professor of Art History
Center for Creative Studies

Checklist of the Exhibition   **Number, Title, Year, Size, Medium.**

No.	Title	Year	Size	Medium
1.	*Restructured photographs,*	1985,	14½ "×12 "	Silverprint
2.	*Restructured photographs,*	1985,	14½ "×12 "	Silverprint
3.	*Restructured photographs,*	1985,	14½ "×12 "	Silverprint
4.	*Restructured photographs,*	1985,	14½ "×12 "	Silverprint
5.	*Restructured photographs,*	1985,	14½ "×12 "	Silverprint
6.	*Restructured photographs,*	1985,	14½ "×12 "	Silverprint
7.	*Restructured photographs,*	1985,	14½ "×12 "	Silverprint
8.	*Restructured photographs,*	1985,	14½ "×12 "	Silverprint
9.	*Restructured photographs,*	1985,	14½ "×12 "	Silverprint
10.	*Restructured photographs,*	1985,	14½ "×12 "	Silverprint
11.	*Restructured photographs,*	1985,	14½ "×12 "	Silverprint
12.	*Restructured photographs,*	1985,	14½ "×12 "	Silverprint
13.	*Restructured photographs,*	1985,	13 "×26 "	Silverprint
1.	*Still Life,*	1986,	14½ "×18½ "	Silverprint
2.	*Still Life,*	1986,	14½ "×18½ "	Silverprint
3.	*Still Life,*	1986,	14½ "×18½ "	Silverprint
4.	*Still Life,*	1986,	14½ "×18½ "	Silverprint
5.	*Still Life,*	1986,	14½ "×18½ "	Silverprint

Statement   **Bill Rauhauser**

In the "Restructured Series" I have attempted to de-emphasize the importance of photographic seeing and reduce the transient element. Selection of subject matter is based not on what it is but rather on what it might become. The shift is from statement to suggestion.

The market presents Phillip Fike,
Bill Rauhauser. Exhibition catalogue
Detroit Artists Market, USA, 1987
Design **Edward Fella**

Und so müssen die Gebäude dastehen.

Wie gebaute Todesengel.

Architektur jetzt

COOP HIMMELBLAU

Die Kausalität steht Kopf.

Architektur ist jetzt.

Book pages. Coop Himmelblau, Germany, 1989

Design Friedhelm Grabowski

Hochschule für Gestaltung

Offenbach

Wir wollen Architektur, die mehr hat.

Architektur muß brennen.

Workspirit. Magazine pages
Vitra, Germany, 1988
Design April Greiman

| W. Amadeus Mozart Symphonie n° 34 |
| Concerto en la Majeur |
| Symphonie n° 39 |

Mozarteum de Salzbourg

Hans Graf Directeur
Edith Preisenhammer Violon

Le Havre
Docks Vauban
Samedi 9 juin. 20h30

Le Mozarteum de Salzbourg ou le gérant de la tradition mozartienne, telle pourrait être un effet l'appellation intégrale de cette formation qui comprend jusqu'à quatre-vingt-onze musiciens tous imprégnés de l'atmosphère de Salzbourg où se fandème de Wolfgang Amadeus. Cette soirée aux Docks Vauban du Havre pourrait aussi s'appeler «Mozart par des mozartiens.

Le Mozarteum fut fondé en 1880 par des professeurs, des élèves et des instrumentistes membres de la «Musique de la Cathédrale», appelée également Mozarteum, désireux de célébrer à Salzbourg les fêtes données en l'honneur de Mozart. C'est donc tout naturellement que l'orchestre prit part au premier festival de Salzbourg en 1920. Bernard Paumgartner confie à l'orchestre les fameuses «matinées Mozart» mais aussi des soirées d'opéra, des concerts de musique de chambre et des concerts spirituels. Encore de nos jours, c'est l'orchestre régulier du devenu très célèbre Festival de Saltzbourg.

En 1939, l'orchestre devient professionnel. Vingt ans plus tard, il sera placé sous l'égide et la protection financière (ndlr. les princes ne faisant plus loi) de la province et de la ville de Salzbourg.

La vie de Wolfgang Amadeus Mozart fut une succession interminable de voyages. L'orchestre, lui aussi, tient à être présent partout dans le monde pour les fêtes en l'honneur de Mozart. La dernière tournée du Mozarteum en France date d'il y a trois ans. C'est un chef viennois, Hans Graf, qui dirige désormais le Mozarteum. Il a fait ses débuts aux opéras de Vienne et de Salzbourg en 1981. Les Français l'ont découvert plus récemment: c'était en 1986 à Aix-en-Provence dans «Idomeneo», puis au Théâtre Musical de Paris, en 1987, dans le cycle Mozart.

Le génie de la musique sera donc pour notre plus grand plaisir interprété par ses serviteurs.

Théâtre des 2 Rives

Alain Bézu Metteur en scène

Le Havre
Docks Vauban
Mardi 12 juin. 20h30
Mercredi 13 juin. 20h30

1984, une grande fête du théâtre se préparait, un peu fou comme les aime le festival et Alain Bézu; après plusieurs années de collaboration entre le Théâtre des 2 Rives et le Festival d'Été, ce projet de monter les trois dernières comédies de jeunesse de Pierre Corneille nécessitait une envie neuve de travailler ensemble. Oui, travailler, car il s'agissait de rassembler toutes les énergies pour que cette idée puisse se réaliser dans la ville de Corneille. Après hésitation, c'est le lycée Corneille, et plus précisément la chapelle, qui fut le décor de ce projet. La suite, nous la connaissons: quelques nuits blanches de théâtre magnifiquement interprétées, la chapelle qui, depuis, a accueilli les meilleures formations musicales du monde.

On ne revit jamais deux fois un projet semblable, mais l'envie était trop forte d'essayer. Nouvelles discussions, nouveaux émerveillements et le projet naît petit à petit. Ce sera «La Place Royale», cinq ans après, pas à Rouen mais au Havre cette fois, et exceptionnellement pour deux soirées dans ces magnifiques publics étonnants, construits en 1850: les Docks Vauban.

La Place Royale de Pierre Corneille

Festival d'été. Programme pages
Festival d'été de Seine-Maritime, France, 1990
Design **Philippe Apeloig**

The new urban landscape. Book contents pages
Olympia & York Companies/Drenttel Doyle. USA, 1988
Design **Drenttel Doyle Partners**

TABLE *of* CONTENTS

Olympia & York Arts
& Events Program
Anita Contini,
Director
Melissa Coley,
Manager
Andrzej Dress,
Design Consultant

Exhibition/Education
Committee
Gary Garrels
Barbara Jakobson
Peter Nagy
Lisa Phillips
Valerie Smith
Philip Yenawine

Exhibition and Catalogue
Contributors
Lisez Reichard
Company, Inc.
Amy Philbin
Coordinator
Anne Blair Wrinkle,
Research

Board of Advisors
David Childs
Mildred Friedman

THE EXHIBITION: TWENTY-
Frank Gehry
Richard Keshack
Richard Martin
Cesar Pelli
Andrée Putman

Catalogue Concept, Design,
and Editorial Consultation
Drenttel Doyle Partners

Catalogue Editor
Richard Martin

Installation Design Concept
David Childs
Frank Gehry
Audrey Matlock

This catalogue documents the exhibition The New Urban Landscape held at The World Financial Center, Battery Park City, New York,
from October 14 through December 31, 1988, sponsored by Olympia & York Companies (U.S.A.).

This exhibition was a part of the program to celebrate the opening of the the public spaces at The World Financial Center.
Printed in the United States of America.
Published 1990 by Olympia & York Companies (U.S.A.) and Drenttel Doyle Partners.
Library of Congress Catalogue Card Number: 89-063218
ISBN: 0.9624916-0-8
Distributed by Rizzoli International Publications, Inc.
300 Park Avenue South, New York, New York 10010

Gegen die Konventionen

Daniel Z.: Ihr repräsentiert – mindestens gegenüber "emigre" – die junge Schweizer Grafik. Oder genauer: Die junge Zürcher Grafik. Das Gemeinsame unter euch, so scheint mir, ist das Gestalten wider die Konvention.

Daniel Z.: You represent – at least for Emigre – young Swiss graphic design. Or, to be precise, young Zurich graphic design. What you have in common, it appears, is design that goes against the grain of convention.

Roland: Konventionen zu überwinden ist schon gut. Aber: Es ist gefährlich, eine visuelle Sprache zu gebrauchen, die letztendlich nur von einem kleinen Kreis Gleichgesinnter oder gar nur noch vom Gestalter selbst verstanden wird. **Daniel Z.:** Wenn es gefährlich ist: Warum machst du es dann? **Roland:** Es gibt verschiedene Ebenen, mit Konventionen zu arbeiten. Wie es auch unterschiedliche Formen gibt, Konventionen zu verweigern oder neue Wege einzuschlagen. Im bildsprachlichen Bereich kann die Konvention im Sinne der Umkehrung, der Satire, der bewussten Vereinnahmung angegangen werden. Daneben gibt es grosse Berührungsflächen, Grenzland sozusagen, zwischen konventioneller Gestaltung und individuellem Anspruch. Wenn ich sage, die individuelle Abweichung von der Konvention könne gefährlich sein, dann will ich damit nicht die Konventionen als unüberwindliche Sprachvoraussetzungen verteidigen. Es geht mir nur darum, das Dogma des Unkonventionellen, Individualistischen gleichermassen in Frage zu stellen. Mir persönlich steht eine dissidente, subkulturelle oder wie auch immer genannte Bildsprache sicher näher als der visuelle Zirkus des spätkapitalistischen Realismus. **Daniel Z.:** Was macht denn die visuelle Verständlichkeit aus? **Polly:** Oft ist die Botschaft eines "normalen" Plakates völlig unverständlich, doch es gibt einen Code zur Verständlichkeit, zum Bild, ja sogar zum Ungestalteten, eine allgemeine Glaubwürdigkeit. **Roland:** Ja, dort, wo mit Konventionen gearbeitet wird, gibt es diese Übereinkunft. Dort funktioniert es. **Polly:** Scheinbar, ja. Deshalb ist es auch gefährlich. Doch – und das ist wohl eine Gemeinsamkeit von uns hier an diesem Tisch – wir sind alle sehr vorsichtig mit dieser scheinbaren Übereinkunft. Das Abbild einer schönen, heilen Naturlandschaft zum Beispiel, die dafür wirbt, für deren Schutz abstimmen zu gehen, weckt in dir das Gefühl, du seist wirklich dort.

Roland: It's all very well to kick against conventions, but it's dangerous to use a visual language that is finally only understood by a small circle of likeminded people – or even only by designers themselves. Daniel Z.: If it's dangerous, why do it? Roland: There are several levels of working in line with conventions. In the same way that there are various ways to go against them and pursue a new direction. In visual language, conventions can be approached in a sense of reversal, or satire. Besides that there are large areas of contact border zones – so to speak, between conventional design and individual claims. When I say individual deviation from convention may be dangerous, I don't mean to defend conventions as an insurmountable prerequisite of language. To me it's only a matter of questioning the dogma of the unconventional and the individualistic. A dissident, subcultural – or whatever you like to call this visual language – is certainly nearer to me personally than a visual circus of late-capitalistic realism. Daniel Z.: So what in fact is visual understanding? Polly: Often the message of the "normal" poster is completely incomprehensible, but there is a code to the understandable, to the illusionary, to the picture, even to the undesigned – a general credibility. Roland: That's right. Wherever one deals with conventions there is this tacit understanding. That's where it functions. Polly: It would seem so. That's why it's also dangerous. And yet – and this is something all of us round this table have in common – we're all very careful with this apparent understanding. The image of a beautiful intact landscape, for instance, is used to advertise its protection and arouses in you the feeling that you are really there.

Wenn wir ein politisches Plakat machen, geht es um den Umstand des Gedruckten: Du stehst vor einem Plakat, das exakt anders sein will als ein Plakat sind das doch so, dass ... Whenever we design a political poster, it's a matter of what is actually printed. You stand in front of a poster that is nothing else but a poster, and that challenges you to act in a certain way. It tells you exactly what is printed, and nothing more.

Richard: You want to elucidate. I don't. To me it's neither a question of bringing across a significant message, nor of being "understood". I don't expect to be understood in the way that I myself understand my visual message. Meine Aufgabe ist es, Wirkung zu erzeugen. Du kannst nicht genau definieren, was und wie der Betrachter deine visuelle Botschaft. **Daniel Z.:** Aber **Richard:** But isn't it precisely your job as designer to make messages understood? **Richard:** My task is to generate an effect. You can't define what exactly, or how the viewer will take in your visual message. There are an endless number of possible ways of looking at it. The only thing I can do as designer is to animate the person through my message. He himself should act, invest, analyze, and reproduce the visual message for himself.

Daniel Z.: Wo ist das, Gestaltung, ist es wohl eine visuelle Botschaft verstehe. **Daniel Z.:** Aber himself. So far me it's more a matter of generating an effect than wanting to teach the viewer anything. ist es nicht deine Aufgabe als Gestalter, Botschaften verständlich zu machen? **Richard:** Meine Aufgabe ist es, Wirkung zu erzeugen. ... The problem is that pictures are interpreted on the symbolic level and not on the factual level of the picture's subject matter.

Richard: So what's the problem?

Daniel Z.: Warum lebst ihr euch gegen diese Art der Betrachtung auf? **Polly:** The great image flood comes from the other side and takes over the language. Popularity is created via a universal understanding of images. If you want to be emancipated and strike against the printed word then you'll quickly become tame. **Daniel V.:** What then is design that makes emancipated reading possible? **Polly:** Because the image flood of our time seems to trivialize. It is an effect due to the reluctance – or incapability – to interpret images on any other level than the subliminal, or unconscious level. A production of images in an impenetrable array of wishes and constraints. Our work is to open up space. Spaces in which you set your text back on the floor. Where not everything is plastered over with pre-digested images.

DARUM auch ist für uns de r TEXT sehr wichtig und die Typographie

DARUM auch ist für uns de r TEXT sehr wichtig
und die Typographie

NÄHE und distanz

WHEN I ACUTALLY WORK FOR

them

That's why text and typography are very important to us. Daniel Z: That may be your personal preference – and I have nothing against the verbal as such – but why can't you counteract this by means of images? Polly: Because images are so charged, because the interpretation of images is done through language rules that are alien to the visual. Roland: Written language makes a higher demand for truth than visual language does. It's more authoritarian. Anyhow, viewed from a totally social aspect – in relation to design – I see it differently. Closeness and distance. Daniel Z: Peter, what's your deeper motivation when you design a concert poster? Peter: There is a fundamental difference for me whether I design a political poster or a concert poster. A concert poster makes hardly any demands. Plus, nobody tells me what to do. With you it's different. You probably have to battle through your concept ... but for me it's to design, to deliver and to get it printed. I guess you have all to engage in deep discussion with the client. I don't have to do that. Daniel Z: But you have clients too who have a close contact with the client. At RecRec I had my workplace in the same room and I was present at many meetings (generally when problems about the business were discussed, not about graphic matters) and I lived together with some of these people. At that time contact with the client was more intensive than it is now. I realize today that I have lost this physical contact and that this also is expressed in my work. Nowadays I get to know the people for whom I work only.

This is not very easy for me. I find it's basically more simple and honest to do graphic design for people I know than for strangers who would quite likely be unsympathetic to me. In large agencies and with big clients the graphic designer no longer has any direct contact with the client. Somebody is engaged specifically for the job of making the contacts. Richard: The fact that a client comes from practically the same background as I do is not important. What is important is that I am able to think on his/her wavelength and that I can accept what he/she does. It is often much better to gain some distance to understand who he and what she wants – about the same distance a psychoanalyst has from his/her patient. Daniel Z: Is the nearness to your client sufficient, Peter? Peter: Well, I do posters this way: I know the music, I leaf through magazines, copy a few pictures – and start. I don't first stop to consider what it is or what should actually be set down. For a political poster I would approach the task in a different way. I would first consider what the message had to be, etc. ... I would probably not do a political poster at all. When I look at all these posters, there is seldom anything that I like – not even those coming from the left. This is sufficient reason for me not to work for them. They're not interested in what I'm doing anyhow, so it's out of the question. It is difficult to experiment in this field. Roland: I see it the same way. It is unimportant for me what the design is for – whether for the opera house, rock music, the museum of design or Citroën. It's far more important what the relationship is between the designer and the client during the design process. This is the point where those designers who make a poster for a rock band, to whose music they are clearly addicted, differ from those whose task is simply to increase sales figures. Peter: I'm not saying that discussions with the client are unimportant to me. But that they have no significant effect on the end result. Polly: The cultural difference to clients often has a productive effect. It spurs you on to do things you otherwise need not do.

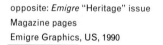

opposite: *Emigre* "Heritage" issue
Magazine pages
Emigre Graphics, US, 1990
Design Richard Feurer
Peter Bäder
Polly Bertram & Daniel Volkart
Roland Fischbacher
Margit Kastl-Lustenberger
Daniel Zehntner

Steelworks. Book pages. Why Not Publishing, UK, 1990. Design Why Not Associates

my head is
still
on

AND THEN, FOR A SECOND, IT WAS AS THOUGH

questions, and I have no television forum to answer the peo
those clubs the first time through. They are four and fourteen
to forgive us and we've asked them to forgive us and our staff who we love so de
able to talk to them. I don't wanna throw any stones, I don't wanna throw an
last newscast we do. I don't know, we don't wanna figh THE WHOLE PLANE WAS OUTLINED
ministry than we really wouldn't want it back anyway."
ALREADY

"Now that the accountants are starting LIKE A NEON SIGN..." that over the past year for example you paid
yourselves, or the board paid you, in salary and dividends and bonusss, a total of 1.9 million dollars. Now that's a far cry from working for nothing,
isn't it?"

Emigre. Magazine pages
Emigre Graphics, USA, 1987
Design Rudy VanderLans

and
continue
to watch
the movie:

AND DATA TAPES.

" I do like to shop, I'm probably well known for my shopping

"Yes, extravagantly! We're just crazy about cars aren't we interested in these
cars?!"   GENER

news. Right **now** with America

"I don't shop for cars and I don't shop for mink coats," PRODUCER, N

and the ou financing on up to a thousand do AYE PR

help my nerves. It AND administration

Combine the cash back offer a special o cars and save

SOMETIMES WOMEN, PEOPLE HAVE A PRIMAL INSTINCTS CRAVING FOR

up to **two thousand one hundred eleven**

HAMBURGERS, SOMETHING HOT, JUICY, AND SO UTTERLY SIMPLE, THAT YOU CAN

dollars on these best selling pickups.

EAT IT WITH YOUR HANDS. I MEAN I KNOW PEOPLE WHO DON'T EAT BURGERS,

Great value programs also offered on most Big board pickups.

BUT I'M NOT SURE I TRUST THEM."

Take advantage of these savings **now!**"

Glenn Suokko, Minneapolis, 6/20-88

Emigre: Who had the idea of acquiring Macintosh computers at Cranbrook? The students or the faculty?

Glenn: We were one of the original three design schools chosen for the Apple/Design School Consortium. Apple generously donated both hardware and software to the Cranbrook Design Department and was very helpful in introducing us to this new phenomenon called the Macintosh. Hugh Dubberly from Apple came out for a few days to help set up the network and offered some valuable training seminars. Kathy and Mike McCoy (CoChairs, Design Department) were very enthusiastic about the possibilities the computer could offer. Many of my classmates had never used a computer before, so it represented not only a new tool to learn, but a new way of working.

Emigre: Were there specific classes taught on the Macintosh?

Glenn: Cranbrook does not teach any technical skills and the program has no formal instruction. For me, the Mac's were a very timely arrival, they arrived the first day of my second year at Cranbrook. Although we had no specific technical training for the Mac, Kathy McCoy assigned design projects that revolved around using the computer, and just by using it, we quickly learned the technical aspects.

Emigre: What did the assignments involve?

Glenn: These projects were designed to explore the Macintosh as a design tool and to see if it would inspire our own design sensibilities in any new or different ways. My particular group did not have specific design assignments using the computer. However, the first-year graphic designers started the program using them. Projects were designed to incorporate many of the software programs, such as PageMaker and Illustrator. There was one particular typographic assignment that we all did, where I set some type, then laser-scanned it and put it into a paint program, printed it out, started it, ran it through the waxer and cut up part of it, xeroxed it, photographed it, laser-scanned it again, and basically ran it through all the technology available in the studio to see what would happen. I let the various technologies take over, and through this process, discovered some interesting formal qualities. We were offered complete freedom in these projects and we were never told we had to use the computer exclusively. Using the Mac at Cranbrook was a matter of choice combined with a lot of encouragement. The computer was available to all of us to use and explore in any way we wanted to. We had no technical instruction at all, but we learned how to use the Mac nevertheless. People who can design pick it up rather quickly. Although some of my classmates resisted it totally, other classmates took to it fairly soon and began to use it exclusively.

Emigre: What did the students who resisted it rebel against?

Glenn: I think the feeling was that the Macintosh could not do anything more than we could using traditional design tools.

Emigre: Do you feel you can do more with it than with traditional methods?

Glenn: The Macintosh is an analogue to our traditional design tools. It is a typesetter, drawing board and mayline, pencil and paint brush, sketch pad, and filing cabinet, but it is all located in one tiny electronic box. I must admit I have become completely addicted to using it. The Macintosh is not much different from the design tools we traditionally use, despite its seemingly progressive capabilities. However, it does allow us firsthand control and the opportunity for endless changes and experimentation.

Emigre: I have seen you use it in a very experimental way. When it comes to type, for instance, you have created new letterforms that are more illustrations than type. Will you continue these experiments?

Glenn: We have all seen the value of the Mac as a production tool and how easy it is to typeset, construct and output final pages, but there are a lot of underexplored possibilities the computer suggests. At Cranbrook, Kathy McCoy really pushed us to explore "the other side" of the computer. I became very interested in developing typography as image, which came out of exploring this "other side." At Cranbrook, we tried to push the computer in different ways by using it unconventionally to

April Greiman Continued

that are wonderful and that I need. I'd like to find an economical way to make the paintbox be more **painterly** and maybe be more **ambiguous** in the final result. Sometimes, **accidentally,** this happens because I am new at it, but I don't feel like I'm really controlling that yet. I'm kind of missing that **painterly feeling that you can get on a Mac.** If you airbrush on the Mac, it's so rough that you always get these wonderful **gestures** out of things, because it is making decisions and approximations at every corner! With the graphic paintbox, the resolution is so high that it's all very accurate, there are no visible approximations. **Emigre:** Will the Macintosh contribute to a change in graphic design mostly in the area of production, or will it influence design aesthetics as well? **April:** Both! In principal, I would agree that the Mac saves us time and all that. But what I experience is rather than doing something quickly, we're **looking at more** possibilities. Instead of doing more work we are **seeing more** options. Now we spend **more time visualizing and seeing things,** and before the Mac, we spent more time doing things. You wouldn't look at twelve different sizes of a headline type, because it would involve setting the type and then statting it and you would just say, "Oh come on, I don't have to try this subtler difference." But with the Mac, once the information is stored, you can just look at seventy-two thousand variations. And then the accidents happen and you say, "Oh that's so much better, why

Glenn Suokko, Back cover Emigre 10.

Glenn Suokko, Detail from Mediate, a typographic experiment.

don't I go that way?" And then you are off on a whole new idea. This pioneering, **where you don't have an aesthetic yet and you don't have tradition,** is both time-consuming and wonderful. **To feel lost is so great.** There are only a few areas in this very controlled industry that you can feel like that. **Emigre:** Where will these experimentations lead to? **April:** There are two ways that we are pushing this technology. One is by **imitating and speeding up normal processes** of different disciplines, such as production and typesetting. Here, the **technology is a slave** and is simulating what we already know. But I think that, if we all keep going the way we are going and other people jump in, all desperate for **new textures/new languages,** then the other area in which it's going to advance is a **new design language.** Rather than get the language that's built-in to speak to you in English, you say, well, I know it can speak English, it does that very well, but there's also a new language. What do digital words really mean and say? There is a **natural language in that machine** and I am interested in finding out what that is, and where the boundaries are. **Emigre:** How come you haven't done any type design on the Macintosh? **April:** There just isn't enough time to do everything. I am such a fanatic about type, and I am so critical and such a perfectionist about it, and there are so many great typefaces that exist. It would take me a year to come up with anything decent and I just don't have the time. **Emigre:** Do you think that there will be an increase in gimmicks and copying due the Macintosh? **April:** Sure, but that happens with any new technology.

I don't worry too much about that. The Mac's so easy to use. It's going to be very scary. It'll be interesting to see what will happen in another three years or so. Kids know how to use this now and everybody will be **modeming** and using **electronic bulletin boards** and what not. So yes, there'll be a lot of mimicry and copying, but it will make the people with traditional design backgrounds and the people with the high-end equipment who know what they are doing push themselves further. For a while, communications may be really ugly and bad. There are going to be large cor-

Wednesday, April 26, 1990, 12.30 PT, Los Angeles

BARRY DECK: Hello?

Emigre: Barry, it's Rudy.

B: Hi.

E: How are you doing?

B: Well, I'm about to run out. I have ten more minutes here and then I have to go and I am sort of in a meeting.

E: I can call back. What would be a good time?

B: Let's say later this afternoon, at three?

E: Fine, I'll call you back at three. Bye.

B: Bye.

Wednesday, April 26, 1990, 3.15 PM, Los Angeles

Barry Deck: Hello?

Emigre: Hi Barry, it's Rudy.

B: I was about to call you. We need to get going if we're going to do this today.

E: Are you on your way out again?

B: No, I'm fine for the next half hour or so.

E: You're a busy man?

B: I guess so.

E: What are you working on?

B: I'm finishing up several pieces for U S West Communications. That's the local telephone company for every state west of Wisconsin with the exception of California.

E: That's a big account!

B: I guess so.

E: Is that a new company?

B: No, I believe they were established when deregulation forced Bell Telephone to split up, one of the Bell babies.

E: Are you working on this all by yourself?

B: I have been. I just came back from the printer with the last of the samples.

E: Did you get a chance to use your own typefaces in it?

B: No, it's all set in Garamond.

E: Why?

B: Oh, this project called for a very refined classical approach, and I haven't worked out my classic font yet.

E: Are you working on one?

B. It's conceptualized but undrawn.

E: I looked at your typefaces and wanted to make some comments.

B. Okay.

E: Well, first of all, I like your typefaces, but I'm not certain why I like them, so I was hoping you'd be able to give me the answer. Even though at closer inspection it is obvious that you are trying to jar these typefaces a little bit, to me they aren't jarred enough. I think most of the faces have interesting details added to what were maybe traditional... click, click...

B. Oh I have a call on the other line.

E. No, don't answer it, don't let them interrupt, I'm taping you. As I was saying, I think most of the faces have interesting details added to what were maybe traditional models, but the diversions are not big enough. When I first saw them, they looked to me like badly drawn versions of existing typefaces.

B. Which ones are you talking about?

E. Right now I'm looking at Barry Sans Serif. But they all suffer from the same problem, except maybe Canicopulis Script and Template Gothic. Although Template Gothic, too, walks this fine line between a badly drawn typeface and... click, click.

B. I have to take this call ...

E. That call waiting is a terrible invention ...

B. I'll be right back ... ! I ... I'm sorry.

E. Do away with it.

B. I don't have a receptionist right now, so whoever calls me has to deal with that.

Barry Sans Serif

ABCDEFGHIJKLMNOPQRSTUVWXYZ
abcdefghijklmnopqrstuvwxyz

Industry Sans Serif

ABCDEFGHIJKLMNOPQRSTUVWXYZ
abcdefghijklmnopqrstuvwxyz

E. Oh. Anyway, in the caps in Template Gothic, it is obvious what you want to accomplish. You have these random thicks and thins. It clearly looks like it's been eaten away by bad reproduction. But that effect is lost in the lower case and the result looks like poor craftsmanship.

B. There are a few things that I tried to accomplish in that particular face. First there is the template reference, which comes partially out of Ed Fella's work, which I'm very much influenced by. It's also an homage to the vernacular. More specifically, there was a sign in the laundromat where I do my laundry. The sign was done with lettering templates and it was exquisite. It had obviously been done by someone who was totally naive. A few months ago, it was replaced with a plastic sign painted by a skilled sign painter. This sign, too, was painted in a naive style, but in another kind of vernacular, the kind that we are more accustomed to seeing these days, so we're not able to fetishize it as easily. I asked them if I could have the old sign, and they gladly handed it over to me. Now it's on the wall in my bedroom.

E. I guess all typeface designers use existing models to style their designs after. Some use old cuts of Garamond and others use laundry signs.

B. I was trying to make it look somewhat as if it had been drawn with a lettering template, but then I also wanted it to look as if it had suffered the distortive ravages of photomechanical reproduction.

E. Why would you want to do that?

B. Well it seems to me that throughout the history of type, type designers have always strived for a certain kind of perfection. Up until today, with some of the recent type designs that I

> I am really interested in type that isn't perfect. Type that reflects more truly the imperfect language of an imperfect world inhabited by imperfect beings.

BARRY DECK.
CONTEMPLATING IMPERFECTION WITH DEAD FLOWERS
AND LAUNDRY SIGN.

have noticed, things have been getting more and more perfect. I am really interested in type that isn't perfect. Type that reflects more truly the imperfect language of an imperfect world inhabited by imperfect beings.

E. But traditional typeface designers are imperfect beings, too, and I'm not sure if drawing perfect typefaces was their one and only goal. First and foremost they spend their lifetimes drawing typefaces that they enjoy creating. But they do it with a great deal of respect for well crafted type and they keep in mind that they're doing this as part of a long tradition of people's reading habits, to which they feel a responsibility to conform.

Emigre. Magazine pages. Emigre Graphics, USA, 1989 (opposite), 1990 (above)

Design Rudy. VanderLans

edged sounding music. The idea of scanning images is in the same mindset as sampling sounds; the only difference is the medium that you're working in. But both methods make it possible to easily manipulate and collage. Laying out a page is pretty much like laying out a sequence of events that make up a song. They both require discipline, order and planning. EMIGRE: Do you ever write your music out at all? JAMES: No. I wish I could though, because that way I could work in the car. That way I could drive to work and scribble down ideas.

"The group He Said (Wire's Graham Lewis with Bruce Gilbert) instantly comes to mind, with Towning's EMIGRE: You can't read or write monotonic vocals, obsessive drum programs, bizarre tape manipulations, and liberal use of music? JAMES: NO. EMIGRE: reverb/echo. Some of these tracks actually follow a verse-chorus structure (albeit loosely) with melodic So how do you start a song? fragments breaking past the mechanical instrumentation on occasion." (Option) JAMES: Mostly trial and error. I usually start with a combination or sequence of notes or some repetitive sample. I can then copy that and change it into a different pitch or tempo, and add more parts to it. Again, it's very much like working on, for instance, a page in Freehand. I do this on an 8-track sequencer/digital synthesizer and a multitude of inexpensive add-on samplers, synthesizers and drum machines. It's not exactly a state-of-the-art setup, but I just keep adding on. I have 8 separate tracks that allow me to record different patterns of sounds simultaneously next to each other. I don't use the drum machines as drum machines. Through the miracle of MIDI (Musical Idiot's Digital Interface), I can play the drum machine noises from the sequencer. That makes it easier to integrate drum noises with other sounds throughout a song. EMIGRE: Do you actually play any other instruments besides keyboards when you are creating these songs? JAMES: No. It's all keyboards. All the "data" is input through a keyboard that's laid out like a piano. The only real contact I have with traditional music-making is those twelve-toned black and white keys. EMIGRE: Do you know how to play the piano, or any other instrument, conventionally? JAMES: No, not conventionally. I have a piano and an old church organ, but I've only sampled and used them as percussion noises or something. (I can play "Chopsticks" and "Heart and Soul" on the piano,) but that's about it. I'm sure that just as a lot of people consider the computer as an invalid way of creating artwork, a lot of musicians consider sequencing as an invalid method of creating music. It's the same argument over and over. Vince Clark once said in an interview something like, "A note is a note, no matter what it's played on." And I agree.

EMIGRE: So you start out with a short pattern. Then what? JAMES: I start layering, building things on it. I have eight tracks of

Pitch catalog cover.

Postcard announcing the release of the Cathode Raymonde cassette.

Cover Cathode Raymonde cassette.

Postcard announcing the release of the Chatterbox cassette.

analog tape that I can record onto. I usually use five or six of them for music, leaving a few for vocals of some accent dialogue or texture of some kind. I often end up using makeshift guitar pedal effects, noise gates, etc. It gets really frustrating sometimes. Like I said before, my studio is certainly far from being state-of-the-art. EMIGRE: Would your music sound significantly different if you had infinite amounts of money to spend on the equipment? JAMES: It would be better. It would be more complex and more precise and the production would be of a higher quality. EMIGRE: Do you feel that's lacking in your work right now? JAMES: No, not really. I think I've come quite a way since I first started. But there's always a lot to learn. The first keyboard I bought was a sampler, and I just taught myself how to use that. Then I kept developing and building. Every couple of months, I usually buy something new, whether it's a used old drum machine from 1980 or whatever. But in general, I'm quite satisfied with the results, considering the equipment that I have. I'm using each piece of equipment to its fullest potential and each has its own qualities. EMIGRE: If any of the established indie

"Towning has quite an ear for sounds and tonalities, flawlessly mixing bass, clavinet, and record companies approached you and said, "We'd like to do a record with you, we have a percussion with droning synth washes, voice and noise." (Option) decent budget, now pick a producer," would you be interested? And whom would you pick? JAMES: I think that would be very interesting. There's a lot of producers that I really respect, like Gareth Jones and Flood and John Fryer and Adrian Sherwood. EMIGRE: Basically the same producers Trent Reznor picked for his Nine Inch Nails record. JAMES: Yes, except I would try to keep my music less predictable. EMIGRE: You don't like that record? JAMES: It can't hold my attention very long, unlike Legendary Pink Dots, The The, He Said, or Severed Heads records. But that's just me. EMIGRE: You are, in a sense, your own producer. If you worked with or worked through someone like John Fryer, do you expect that it would change your music? JAMES: I've never worked with a producer, so I'm not sure how much input they would have. I was just looking at it from a standpoint that if someone took what I've recorded, mixed it, and added their little tricks of the trade, it would enhance the end result, and I wouldn't have to deal with the whole mixing thing alone. EMIGRE: So there's still a lot to be learned? JAMES: Oh, yes. And to me the most frustrating part of creating music is either the singing or the mixing. Those are the two most organic processes in recording music. They happen in real time. I find it easy to sit down and program something to a point where it is exact and all I have to do is hit the start button to record it. But then, when I have to mix it, it's an altogether new game. You can do twenty mixes of something and still not get it right.

EMIGRE: What do you think of the rising status of producers? Their credits are getting bigger and bigger and some records sell better because a certain producer has their name on it. JAMES: I don't think their work has changed much. Maybe the world is becoming a bit more receptive to or aware of what they're doing. I know I always look at the producer's name on the back of a record before buying it. Producers do great things with other people's music. What puzzles me is how satisfying can it be to be a producer and not play music yourself? It's like art directors or production persons who don't design anything themselves. If I were a great producer, I'd be out there making my own music. EMIGRE: Well, aren't you? JAMES: Yes, I guess I am. Not a great producer, but at least I'm producing my own music. I could be completely wrong about the role producers have though, they could all be closet rock stars.

EMIGRE: If you had to give up one or the other, which would you choose to do, the graphic design work or the music? JAMES: I like doing both, but I get more out of the music because I find it more difficult to create. I'd love to eventually be able to integrate the two more, maybe through video or computer animation. I'm investigating the creative advantages of sequencing and recording on the Macintosh, and if I decide to go with that,

Mac-animation software will be next.

Emigre. Magazine pages
Emigre Graphics, USA, 1990 (above), 1991 (opposite). Design Rudy VanderLans

A CONVERSATION WITH

Edward Fella

AND

Mr. Keedy: You were trained as a commercial artist and illustrator and worked in various commercial art studios in Detroit. After 30 years in a successful career, why did you go to school, first at Center for Creative Studies and then to Cranbrook?

Fella: One reason was I had spent all these years in the commercial art business and I never felt I was really "legitimate." So I thought if I went to school, getting a degree would somehow legitimize what I did. By this time, design degrees were quite prevalent in the profession. Another reason was that it would give me the option to teach.

Mr. Keedy: These were not really considerations when you started your career?

Fella: Not at all. I went to Cass Technical High School. I never attended a university. Despite being offered a scholarship when I graduated, I didn't go, because I received such good training as a commercial artist in high school, I entered the art business immediately and became a practicing professional by the time I was nineteen. In the fifties, going to school and having a degree, especially with my Detroit working class background, wasn't that important. Being able to work was. Years later, I came to regret that. By the mid-eighties, I had another opportunity to go to school. My children were grown up, about to leave home to go to college, and I thought, "*Wow*, why don't I do the same thing? Then I won't feel this kind of separation anxiety." I had spent the last fifteen years bringing up my children as a single parent, all while working of course. Which is easy to do in the design/art business, since you make your own time and hours and determine your own income.

Mr. Keedy: Going to graduate school at the age of 48 was also easier for you because you happened to be friends with Kathy McCoy?

Fella: Right, that was another connection. In the late sixties, I was working as a designer/illustrator at Skidmore Sahratian, a Detroit art studio, when Kathy McCoy was

hired on as a designer. She was different **Mr. Keedy** from most of the other people I'd known in the art business, because she had actually studied design in college, whereas most of my peers hadn't. Though we were all very successful commercial artists, most of us had either technical high school backgrounds or had come up through the apprentice system, a sort of on-the-job training. Kathy studied industrial design, and then she went on to work as a graphic designer for various corporations. Through her I became more involved in an analytical

approach to design than I had ever considered before. This approach was more typical of academic, "pure" graphic design... What I opened up for Kathy, which later fed into the program at Cranbrook, was an understanding and sympathy for the "low end" of commercial art and the vernacular. This happened at the same time as the transition between Modernism and Post-Modernism, and the influence of the Venturi books. In the studio, we commercial designers would kid Kathy about her high design background, and she would kid us back, but we developed a common respect that really changed my own practice and made it much more considered. It helped me put the

design part of my own work into a sort of historical perspective, which I hadn't connected before. In commercial art studios, illustrators like myself were very aware of the history of illustration and knew some design history too. I knew the Museum of Modern Art version of the history of design, Futurism, Dada, the Bauhaus. Like a lot of other advertising designers, I wasn't aware of the ideas behind later versions of Modernism, like Swiss Design; I thought it was just another style. It really didn't mean much to us because we weren't corporate designers and we weren't involved in design systems. But we did recognize the stylistic

signs of that work. This was in 1969 or 1970.

Mr. Keedy: The vernacular is a very hot issue in graphic design today. However, most graphic designers think and use the vernacular differently from you, since you came out of commercial art.

Fella: I was the vernacular! I was like those people that Robert Venturi wrote about, right? The guys that made the signs in Las Vegas. On a somewhat higher level of course, kind of a mid-level of vernacular. It wasn't the folk vernacular, which commercial artists were very fond of. We all read *GRAPHIS* and articles about various kinds of folk art and signs. Since I was also a decorative illustrator, I was especially interested in things that were crude or naive, unlearned, because that is what decorative illustration took so much inspiration from.

Mr. Keedy: When you entered Cranbrook, and were really immersed in "high design," did it change the way you thought about the vernacular and what it means? You could have just completely dumped the vernacular and become a sophisticated Modernist designer.

Fella: I guess I could have, but I was too cynical for that. I saw this "high end" design being as much a style as the various vernaculars.

Mr. Keedy: So you are interested in them equally then?

Fella: Yes, and one of the things I wanted to bring to "high design" was the vernacular or commercial art, which had had a really bad name, as did advertising, since the sixties. Somehow graphic design was considered to be more pure, despite it's connection to the corporate world. Today, corporate, Swiss (International Style) graphic design has a bad name, like commercial art or advertising design had twenty years ago, which is kind of ironic.

Mr. Keedy: You have a lot of polaroids of signs. And have been collecting examples of the vernacular for a

Type catalogue. The Netherlands, 1990, Design Max Kisman

Beach culture. Magazine pages
Surfer Publications, USA, 1991 (top), 1990 (bottom)
Art director David Carson

summer's here
JUNE 19,

o get some culture and check out:

two faces for the 90's—john wesley harding (singer-songwriter) . beach culture magazine.

Santa Monica pier

plus the usual mix of art, places, st yle

the ULTIMATE A sport

rd st

h book

RFSHOPS

st.
h
that
at
anging
≈ minu
hanging at
c ar ging
carmine st.

The year is 1979. And 1942. At a small neighborhood pool in Greenwich Village, a movie crew is time-tripping 30-odd years into the past to film "Raging Bull," the story of boxer Jake LaMotta. A gang of skinny, shirtless kids holler from a rooftop as the cameras follow Robert DeNiro (playing LaMotta). He buys a soda at the concession stand, and sits at a picnic table with the actor playing LaMotta's brother. Around the pool, women in one-piece bathing suits relax in chaise lounges, and local Mafia hoods in tropical shirts play cards. DeNiro has eyes for only one: the platinum blonde who sits at pool's edge, luxuriantly paddling her long legs in the cool water. The camera moves in for a close-up of her legs...and director Martin Scorsese calls,

Beach culture. Magazine pages
Surfer Publications, USA, 1991 (left), 1990 (right)
Art director David Carson

FEATURE

GRAPHIC

letters 9

TYPE

PURE

IMM PURE

[ver -nak-yoo- ler]

Perfo 3. Poster. Lantaren Venster, The Netherlands, 1985
Design Hard Werken

Doorbraak (Breakthrough). Exhibition poster. Damrak Amsterdam, The Netherlands, 1989
Design: The Thunder Jockeys

wenst u een *gelukkig*

opposite:

Intomart wenst u een gelukkig 1986 (Intomart wishes you a happy 1986). Best wishes card. Intomart, The Netherlands, 1986
Design: Ton van Bragt Studio Dumbar
Photography: Lex van Pieterson

European illustration. Book pages. Booth-Clibborn Editions, UK, 1989
Design: The Thunder Jockeys
Photography: Peter Ashworth

16th

89-90

European Illustration

ⓒ edited by Edward Booth-Clibborn ⓒ

edité par Edward Booth-Clibborn

— herausgegeben von Edward Booth-Clibborn —

jury

Michel de Boer

Jerry Hibbert

Mary Lewis

Richard Markell

Deld Stamenkovits

Brian Webb

Current work from artists studios
Poster/mailer. Detroit Focus Gallery, USA, 1987. Design Edward Fella

Vickie Arndt/Peter Lenzo
Poster/mailer. Detroit Focus Gallery, USA, 1990. Design Edward Fella

opposite:
European illustration. Book page
Booth-Clibborn Editions, UK, 1989. Design The Thunder Jockeys

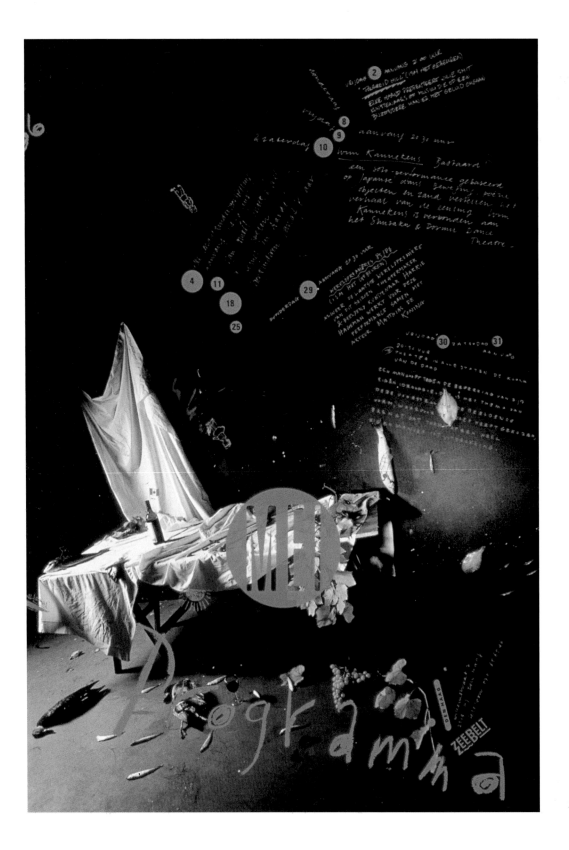

Mei programma. Programme poster
Zeebelt theatre, The Netherlands, 1986
Design Linzi Bartolini
Gert Dumbar
Esther Vermeer
Studio Dumbar
Photography: Lex van Pieterson

James Surls. Exhibition poster
Cranbrook Academy of Art Museum, USA, 1987
Design David Frej

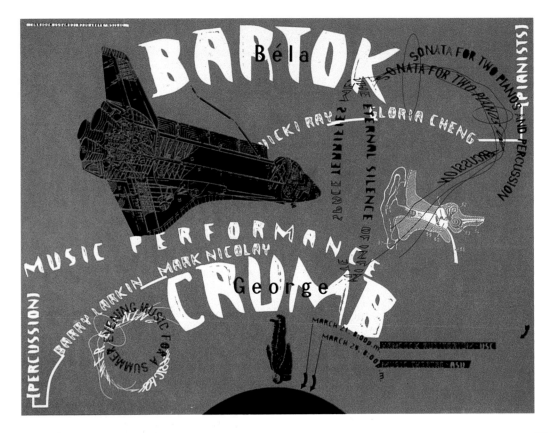

above: Poster. USA, 1989. Design Barry Deck

Nu-bodies. Poster/flyer. Detroit Focus Gallery, USA, 1987. Design Edward Fella

above: Postcard. Artworks, USA, 1988
Design Jeffery Keedy

Excavator-Barcelona-Excavador. Pages from an artist's book. UK, 1986. Design Jake Tilson

opposite: *Continuum.* Poster/mailer
Detroit Focus Gallery, USA, 1990
Design Edward Fella

Reception: FRIDAY, Oct. 12th, from 5:30-8:30 PM
Oct 12 - Nov. 10th 1990

CONTINUUM

AVERY BOONE
JAMES H. DOZIER
MARIA-THERESA FERNANDES

RUTH LAMPKINS
RICHARD LEWIS
STEVEN MEALY

AARON IBN PORI PITTS

REGINALD GAMMON
ESDRAS M. SANTIAGO

CURATORS
GILDA Snowden
LESTER Johnson

DETROIT
FOCUS GALLERY
743 Beaubien   3rd fl.
DETROIT, MI 48226
tel. 313 962-9025
hrs: WED-SAT. 12-6 P.M.

169

Artemisia Gallery
Chicago Artists Spaces
Poster/mailer
Detroit Focus Gallery, USA, 1987
Design Edward Fella

opposite:
i-D. Magazine pages
Terry Jones/Tony Elliot, UK, 1990
Art director Stephen Male Nice

Lisa Anderson *(BMG/RCA)*, Norman Cook *(Beats International)*, Dave Dorrell *(ex- M/A/R/R/S/, DJ, remixer)* Boy George *(Jesus Loves You)*, MC Mell'O' *(UK rapper)* and Tony Wilson *(Factory Records /media mouth)*.

Chaired by John Godfrey

WHAT DO YOU THINK THE BIGGEST PROBLEM FACING THE RECORD INDUSTRY IS NOW?
TONY WILSON Personally, the problem for the British record industry now is breaking the Brash scene in America.
NORMAN COOK Is it such a big deal?
BOY GEORGE Financially.
TONY WILSON Financially, yeah. It makes an enormous fucking difference financially.
BOY GEORGE Is there anyone making money out of dance music in this country?
LISA ANDERSON and **TONY WILSON** No unsong? Yes.
TONY WILSON If you get albums out of it - no-one makes money out of dance music per se if it remains 12" single orientated, only if you have an album going.
DO YOU THINK THE BRITISH SCENE TODAY HAS ANY SIMILARITIES TO THE '60S?
TONY WILSON Yeah, drugs.
NORMAN COOK Is it that simple?
BOY GEORGE I think it is drugs.
DAVE DORRELL Everyone is giving it hippy this and that, but they're all mods really, they should all be wearing straight suits.
TONY WILSON But none of them were born in the '60s. When everyone tried to revive psychedelia, like the Liverpool bands tried to do in '81/'82, it didn't work. It could only really happen again when young people hadn't experienced it. And there's an unselfconsciousness to it now which was never there in the '60s, and that's what makes it new.
BOY GEORGE I think all it is is the drugs that have got a lot of normal kids from the suburbs into music that they probably won't even into before, there's a lot of people dancing now who weren't into music before.
NORMAN COOK But they don't think they're into music.
TONY WILSON Course they are, course they are, course they are!
NORMAN COOK I think they're into it through fashion.
TONY WILSON Noel!
BOY GEORGE And I think the record companies are just destroying everything.
LISA ANDERSON Here we go, here we go.
BOY GEORGE They are, they are destroying everything.
LISA ANDERSON Thankyou George.
THE 'SIGN UP ANYTHING FROM MANCHESTER' MENTALITY?
LISA ANDERSON Certainly not.
TONY WILSON We'll sell anything.
LISA ANDERSON I wouldn't sign anything from Manchester, anyway it's all been signed up.
TONY WILSON If you think it's going to make money, and clearly several people think that the new scene is going to make money ...
LISA ANDERSON It's going to make money for someone.
TONY WILSON It's making money already, and as I said, the only problem left is if it breaks in America, cos if it does it will make an awful lot of money for everybody.
DAVE DORRELL Do you think it will?
TONY WILSON Er, 60/40 - about the same odds as keeping the Hacienda open, slightly more than even.
BOY GEORGE I don't know if America's that into it though.
TONY WILSON But it depends if they're going to wake up. *The kids who were buying Jason and Kylie two years ago are now 11, and 11 year olds are buying Stone Roses, Happy Mondays and the rest of it.* And if that's happening in Britain, one has to wonder if American kids who are buying New Kids On The Block now, in a year's time they're going to be older and they're going to see this exciting stuff coming out of this country.
NORMAN COOK Well let's face it, if 11 year old English kids can cope with The Happy Mondays, 20 year old Americans must be able to, mustn't they?
LISA ANDERSON Not necessarily. They're so susceptible to what is sold to them.
NORMAN COOK I reckon Americans are hung up on the whole dream of rock'n'roll, the James Dean element. I don't think they can cope with anything unless it has the essential rock'n'roll ingredient.

Pete Ayrton *(Serpent's Tail)*, Michael Bracewell *(novelist)*, Christopher Fowler *(horror writer)*, Giles O'Brien *(4th Estate)* and Mike Phillips *(crime writer)*.

Chaired by Steve Beard and Jim McClellan

What do you think the Booker Prize represents and is it desirable?
MIKE PHILLIPS I don't have anything against the Booker Prize. Unfortunately I don't think I'm going to get it. But does it represent a kind of oppressive literary culture? I don't think that it does in itself. I think it reflects a literary culture that comes out of a static notion that the country has of itself, never mind literature. And I think the reason that can be oppressive, if it's oppressive at all, is because we haven't yet begun to reassemble the elements of an English or British identity and understand it. So in a way, the whole superstructure that's represented by the Booker Prize and the publishers and all the rest of it is, in a sense, *alien* to lots of people writing now. Because it doesn't share the identity that they're describing and assembling in Britain now.
CHRISTOPHER FOWLER It represents a sort of stratified upper middle class, and it's almost a genre in itself, in that you can classify a book as a Booker book. It's almost as if the books are being chosen for the ability to find some permanence in some pantheon of future literature. It seems to be very narrow, and it keeps dangerously away from anything realistic, or too much outside of what the average person who sees the little sticker on the shelves saying 'Booker Prize short-listed', experiences.
MIKE PHILLIPS You can see the style - it's the sort of book that when you open it you think, *Oh shit this is going to be really hard to read.*
GILES O'BRIEN You've got to remember that the reason that money is there is that Booker want to see their name on those nice little printed plaques that go round with the books. Each year it's a completely different set of six judges, mind you these people are chosen cos they represent some kind of literary establishment, and I think they feel a pressure to represent that establishment. But I think they also feel a pressure to produce a popular winner, one that people will actually read and enjoy. And that is because it is a marketing exercise, it's not conceived as a literary exercise, it's very useful for publishers, it's very useful for Booker - although I don't actually know what Booker do other than sponsor the Booker Prize.
MIKE PHILLIPS I'll tell you what Booker has done - *Booker owned my country.* The country where I was born, Guyana, you walk down the high street and everything says Booker, Booker, Booker. I've always found it slightly galling to come here, and to find that Booker is handing out money in this way.
PETE AYRTON To be fair it's changing, and to a certain extent the way it's changing is reflected by the jury and who's chosen, and the things we're doing and other people are publishing. I mean, last year Maggie Gee and Ed White were on the jury, this year Kate Saunderson, and James Kelman was short-listed last year - these are steps forward. You know, one's looking at it as if it's this dead weight that every year comes up with Anita Brookner, which happens some years, but it is changing, and to a large extent it depends on who's in the jury. To what extent they will continue to get interesting and non-mainstream people onto the jury though, one doesn't know; but it's the book trade that is the first to complain. When Keri Hulme won, the New Zealand feminist novelist, it was the book trade who complained cos they couldn't sell the book. The problem is the book shops, not Booker or the people who select the book.
CHRISTOPHER FOWLER So are there some books which the audience would buy if it won the Booker?
GILES O'BRIEN Yeah, it makes a tremendous difference.
PETE AYRTON But I think that one can get too hung up on this thing - obviously it's been good for books, it's been good for writers, it gets TV coverage, it raises the profile of books and makes this country more book conscious, which God knows, you know...
MICHAEL BRACEWELL I agree with Pete, also the fact that Kelman and Banville got on the short-list last year - I thought that was very much a step in the right direction. I have this sneaking suspicion that any of us who wrote couldn't help but feel rather pleased.
PETE AYRTON And everybody's doing it now - The Sunday Express have got one, Whitbread have got one - it can't be bad, all these people throwing money at writers.
CHRISTOPHER FOWLER The Sunday Express have got one?!
PETE AYRTON Yeah, I think it's the richest, and there's one in Ireland, the Guinness one, which is £50,000.
CHRISTOPHER FOWLER *I didn't think the people who read The Sunday Express bought books, I thought they watched TV.*

Are genre writers perceived as being on the margins of literature? ♦

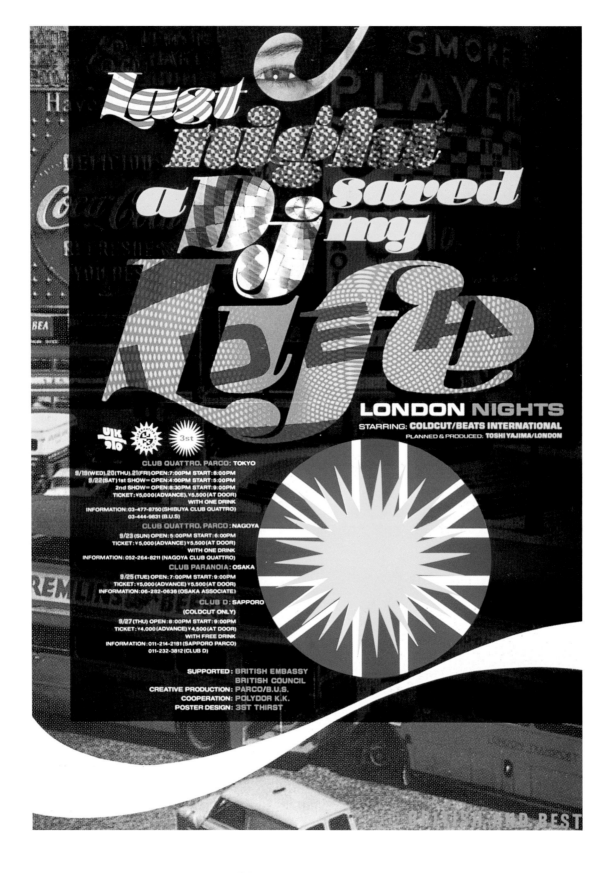

Last night a DJ saved my life. Club poster. Parco, Tokyo, 1990

Design Richard Bonner-Morgan, Neil Edwards, Stephen Male Nice

Madstock . . . Advertisement. Candyflip, UK, 1990

Design Neil Edwards Nice

173

Wise up sucker. 12" single cover (back)
RCA, UK, 1989
Design Designers Republic

opposite: *This is the day . . . this is the hour . . . this is this!*
Album cover (back). RCA, UK, 1989
Design Designers Republic

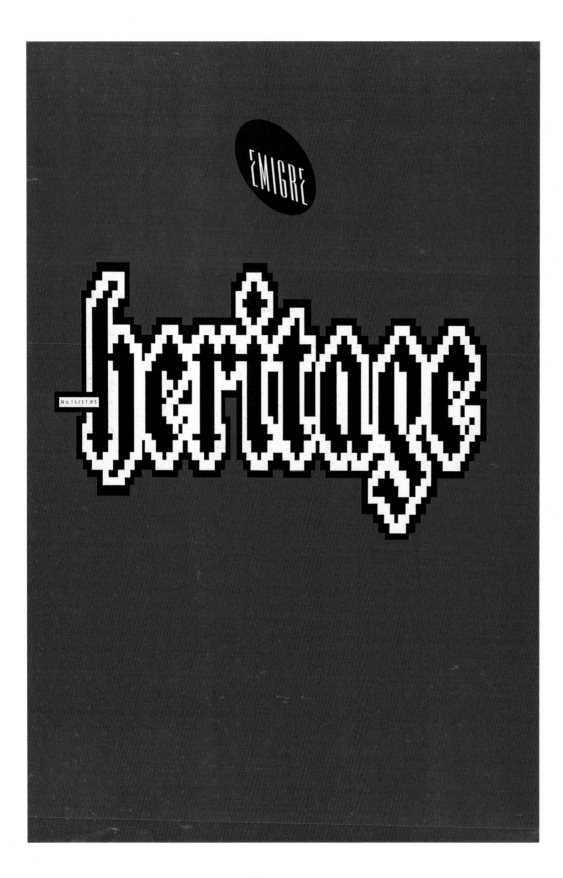

opposite:

Emigre. Magazine cover. Emigre Graphics, USA, 1990

Design Rudy VanderLans

Tegentonen. Concert poster. Paradiso Amsterdam,
The Netherlands, 1986

Design Max Kisman

below: *Breakfast Special*
Pages from artist's book. UK, 1989
opposite: *Excavator-Barcelona-Excavador*
Pages from an artist's book. UK, 1986
Design Jake Tilson

ENTRADA

Núm.

ENTRADA

Núm.

ENTRADA

Soil and plant traces

"Place of discharge (and examination if different)"

"SHOOT THE AMERICAN SPY!"

400 years later...

BARCELONA

Error
Codes

On the glass splinters that were found, there was the same break
co-efficient as in the glass remaining in the window of the bar.

Agent's No _____

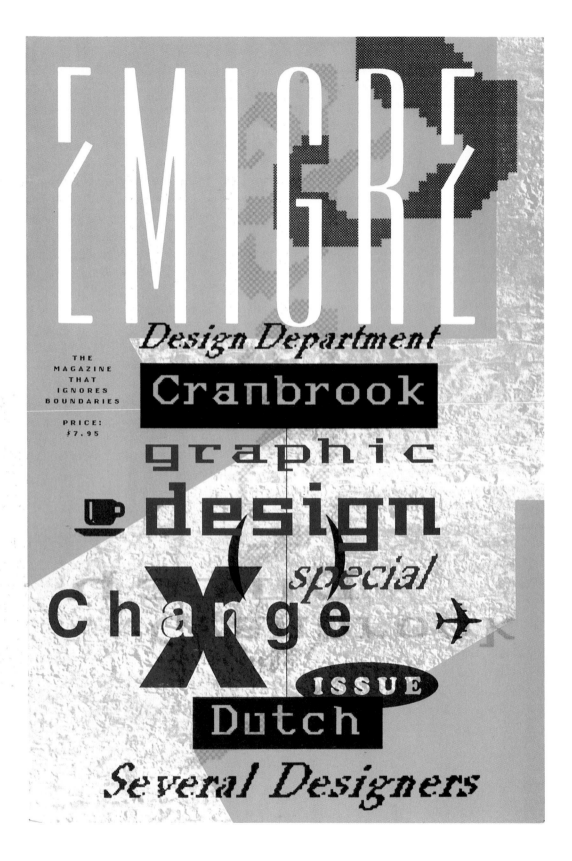

EMIGRE

THE
MAGAZINE
THAT
IGNORES
BOUNDARIES

PRICE:
$7.95

Design Department

Cranbrook

graphic

design

special

Change

X

ISSUE

Dutch

Several Designers

opposite:

Emigre. Magazine cover. Emigre Graphics, USA, 1988
Design Glenn Suokko

Binary race. Booklet. Emigre Graphics, USA, 1991
Design/photography Rudy VanderLans

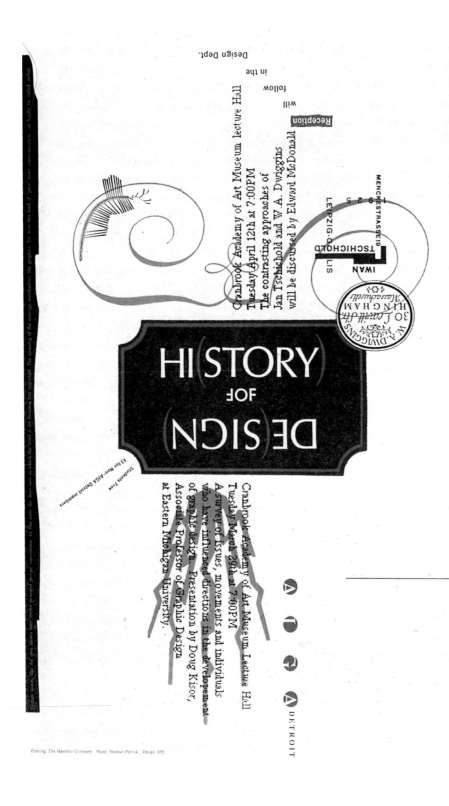

History of design/story of sign. Poster/mailer
American Institute of Graphic Arts Detroit, USA, 1988. Design Edward McDonald

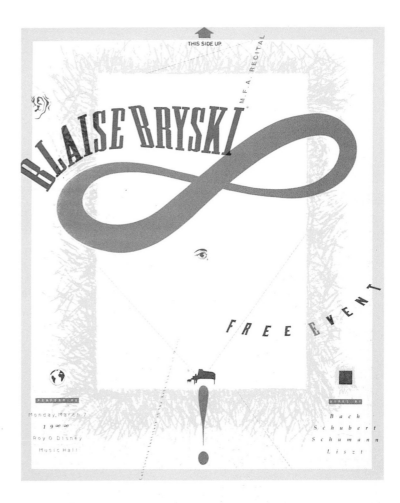

above:

Blaise Bryski. Concert poster. California Institute of the Arts, USA, 1988. Design Barry Deck

below:

Fournier le jeune. Poster. USA, 1985. Design Edward McDonald

Cranbrook Academy of Art

L'âge typographique (The age of typography). Poster. France, 1989
Design Philippe Apeloig

Visual arts department. Folder. Arts Council, UK, 1991

Design Why Not Associates

in

A B C D E F G H
a b c d e f g h
I J K L M N O P Q
i j k l m n o p q
R S T U V W X Y Z
r s t u v w x y z
1 2 3 4 5 6 7 8 9 0

Industria Inline. Linotype, UK, 1990
opposite: *Arcadia.* Linotype, UK, 1990
Design Neville Brody

ustria

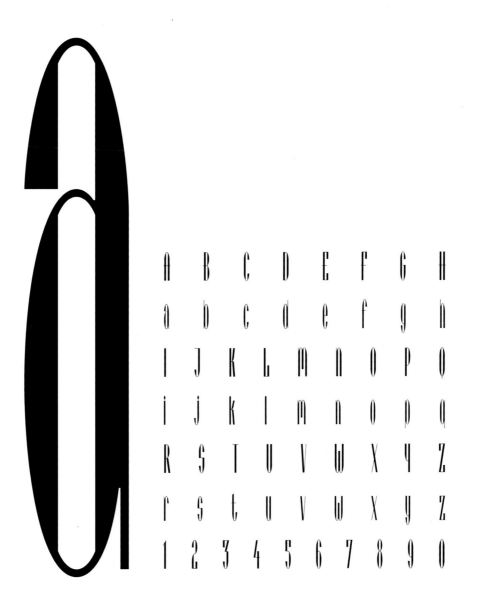

A B C D E F G H
a b c d e f g h
I J K L M N O P
i j k l m n o p
R S T U V W X Y Z
r s t u v w x y z
1 2 3 4 5 6 7 8 9 0

rcadia

o

a

k

ABCDEFGH
abcdefgh
IJKLMNOPQ
ijklmnopq
RSTUVWXYZ
rstuvwxyz
1234567890

Oakland Ten. Emigre Graphics, USA, 1985. Design Zuzana Licko

a

Matrix Regular. Emigre Graphics, USA, 1986. Design Zuzana Licko

matri

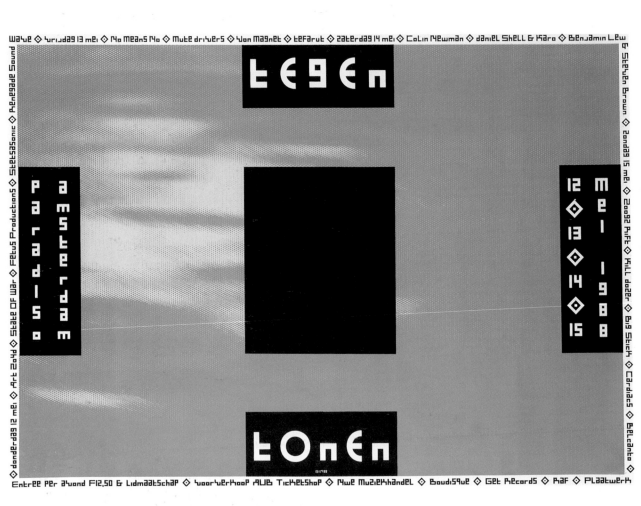

above:
Concert poster. Application of Tegentonen
Paradiso Amsterdam, The Netherlands, 1988

Tegentonen. The Netherlands, 1988-90
Design Max Kisman

ABCDEFGH

abcdefgh

IJKLMNOPQ

ijklmnopq

RSTUVWXYZ

rstuvwxyz

1234567890

Modular Regular. Emigre Graphics, USA, 1985. Design Zuzana Licko

A B C D E F G H

a b c d e f g h

I J K L M N O P Q

R S T U V W X Y

r s t u v w x y z

1 2 3 4 5 6 7 8 9 0

Zwart Vet. The Netherlands, 1987 (capitals), 1990 (lowercase and special characters). Design Max Kisman

Scratch Regular. FontShop "FontFont" series, The Netherlands, 1990. Design Max Kisman

Vortex. FontShop "FontFont" series, The Netherlands, 1990. Design Max Kisman

ABCDEFGH
abcdefgh
IJKLMNOPQ
ijklmnopq
RSTUVWXYZ
rstuvwxyz
1234567890

lunati

Lunatix Bold. Emigre Graphics, USA, 1988. Design Zuzana Licko

A B C D E F G H

a b c d e f g h

I J K L M N O P Q

i j k l m n o p q

Triplex Italic Bold. Emigre Graphics, USA, 1985. Design John Downer

R S T U V W X Y Z

r s t u v w x y z

1 2 3 4 5 6 7 8 9 0

slim

Jacque Slim, Regular and Fat. FontShop, The Netherlands, 1990. Design Max Kisman

regular

A B C D E F G H
a b c d e f g h
I J K L M N O P Q
i j k l m n o p q
R S T U V W X Y Z
r s t u v w x y z
1 2 3 4 5 6 7 8 9 0

Fat

Brokenscript Bold. FontShop "FontFont" series, The Netherlands, 1991
Design Just van Rossum

ABCDEFGH
abcdefgh
IJKLMNOPQ
ijklmnopq
RSTUVWXYZ
rstuvwxyz
1234567890

Totally Gothic. Emigre Graphics, USA, 1990
Design Zuzana Licko

200 PT.   150 PT.   72 PT.   48 PT.   36 PT.   18 PT.

A B C D E F G H I K

L M N O P Q R S

T U V W X Y Z

a b c d e f g h i j k l m n o p q r s t u v w x y z

Spindly Bastard. UK, 1990. Design Jonathan Barnbrook

Posters. Applications of Bastard. UK, 1990
Design Jonathan Barnbrook

THiS iS PROTOTYPE. EACH LETTER iS UPPER AND LOWER CASE SERiF AND SANS SERiF. THE LETTERFORMS ARE CREATED BY COLLAGiNG PARTS FROM ABOUT TEN OTHER TYPEFACES iNCLUDiNG GiLL, PERPETUA, FUTURA AND BEMBO. iT WAS iMPORTANT TO KEEP ALL THE COMPONENTS THE SAME TO EMPHASiSE THAT iT WAS 'BROUGHT TOGETHER' ON A COMPUTER RATHER THAN HAND DRAWN

ABCDEFGHiJKLMN OPQRSTUVWXYZ

1234567890

Prototype. UK, 1990. Design Jonathan Barnbrook

opposite: *Fudoni Bold Remix.* The Netherlands, 1991. Design Max Kisman

ABCDEFGH
abcdefgh
IJKLMNOPQ
ijklmnopq
RSTUVWXYZ
rstuvwxyz
1234567890

oni

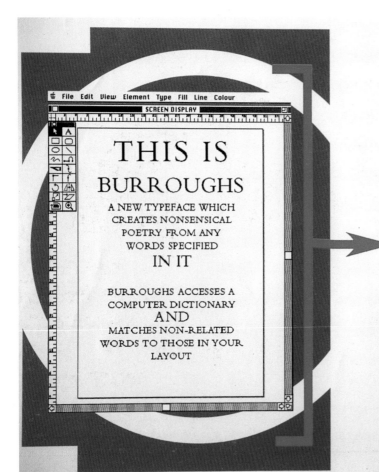

PRINTER OUTPUT

LARD GUN

CATHODE

REFER KNUCKLE IRATE
LINT ELSEWHERE
JOB BERLIN SCRAPE
FORTITUDE SMALL

CHINTZ HAM

CURVET INDICATOR HOME
OZONE LIMB
REMIND
KITSCH ELSEWHERE
INFORM IN CONTOUR FLASH
INVALID

above: *Burroughs*. UK, 1991. Design Jonathan Barnbrook

Beowolf 23. Random font. FontShop, The Netherlands, 1990. Design Erik van Blokland Just van Rossum

ABCDEFGH
abcdefgh
IJKLMNOPQ
i j k l m n o p q
RSTUVWXYZ
rstuvwxyz
1234567890

opposite: *Boem Paukeslag Remix.* Poster
Application of Extended Maxm!x
Typ/Typografisch Papier, The Netherlands, 1991. Design Max Kisman

BOEM

PAUKESLAG

PLAT

daar ligt alles

0 ————————————— 0

weer razen violen cell bassen koperen triangel

trommels PAUKEN

razen rennen razen rennen razen RENNEN

drama in volle slag hoeren slangen werpen zich op eerlijke

mannen het gezin wankelt de fabriek wankelt

de eer wankelt ligt er

alle begrippen VALLEN

HALT!

Repressed Victorian Roman

(A B C D E F G H I J K L M N O P Q R S T U V W X Y Z)

[a b c d e f g h i j k l m n o p q r s t u v w x y z]

(ABCDEFGHIJKLMNOPQRSTUVWXYZ) [1 2 3 4 5 6 7 8 9 0]

[abcdefghijklmnopqrstuvwxyz]

[1234567890]

JOHN RUSKIN

Although his theories regarding architecture and society have been widely read and accepted as the seeds of the modern movement, John Ruskin's bizarre fear of sexual activity haunted him for many years. These horrors, although shrouded in secrecy throughout his lifetime, and by his principal biographers, are confirmed in a series of letters and diary entries found, long after his death, under a floor board in his study. After marrying Effie Gray, who was born in the room in which Ruskin's grandfather had committed suicide, he declared her "unfit for consumation", adding that he would reconsider when she reached the age of twenty-five she was twenty-eight and she was nineteen. Six years later, on her twenty-fifth birthday, Ruskin had still not reckoned with his legendary disdain for pubic hair, and told her that she was still unfit, citing religious reasons for his abstention. Quite shortly after, the marriage was anulled, and Effie was remarried to the Pre-Raphaelite painter, John Millais.

above: *Repressed Victorian Roman.* USA, 1989

opposite top: *Canicopulus Script.* USA, 1989

opposite: *Barry Sans Serif.* USA, 1989   Design Barry Deck

Caricopulus Script

(ABCDEFGHIJKLMNOPQRSTUVWXYZ

[abcdefghijklmnopqrstuvwxyz]

[1234567890]

(ABCDEFGHIJKLMNOPQRSTUVWXYZ)
[abcdefghijklmnopqrstuvwxyz]
[1234567890]

Eric Gill

BARRY SANS SERIF

(A B C D E F G H I J K L M N O P Q R S T U V W X Y Z)
[a b c d e F g h i j k l m n o p q r s t u v w x y z]
{ 1 2 3 4 5 6 7 8 9 0 }

(ABCDEFGHIJKLMNOPQRSTUVWXYZ)
[abcdeFghijklmnopqrstuvwxyz]
{1234567890}

BARRY DECK

The latest Force to rear its ugly head on the ever unfolding continuum of the postscript font design Frontier, Former disciple of the infamous rectorial school and recent absorbaten of autotrace typography, is Barry Deck. He cuts his punches in a Frenzy of mouse clicks and key commands, producing a major Flow of vector based bezier curve coordinates which are infinitely re-producible. Fueled by almost two grueling years of damn-nearly continuous sexual frustration as a graduate student at California Institute of the Arts, he designs Fonts which combine influences From the past with lewd references to the boundless-ness of his own lust (as Focused on Fetishized typo-graphical Form), and the vital energy and singleminded internal and external drive necessary to blow these little characters right out of the laserwriter and into the Future. Held in his hand For days at a time, the indispensable mouse becomes an extension of the phallus, and the outcome re-produces itself in endlessly reconfiguring or-gies of language and dyslexic "FluFFe-mes" on the printed page. The typefaces produced under these conditions, with this methodology, exhibit the sort of spon-taneity and passion that exists within sexuality itself. A combination oF all Barry relishes in typography, Barry Sans SeriF is one such Face.

ABCDEFGHIJKLMN
OPQRSTUVWXYZ
abcdefghijklmnop
qrstuvwxyz
[1234567890]
№ @ ! % $ & ?

ABCDEFGHIJKLMN
OPQRSTUVWXYZ
abcdefghijklmnop
qrstuvwxyz
[1234567890]
№ at ! % $ AND & ?

Template Gothic. USA, 1990. Design Barry Deck

Surfer. Magazine pages. Application of Template Gothic and Industry Sans Serif
Surfer Publications, USA, 1991. Art director David Carson

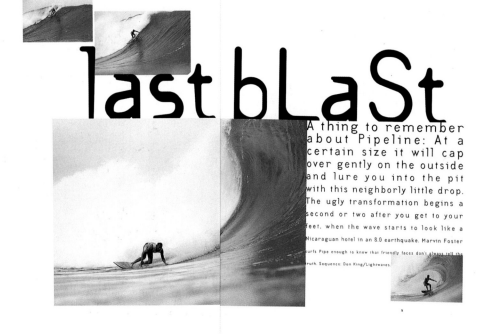

last bLaSt

A thing to remember
about Pipeline: At a
certain size it will cap
over gently on the outside
and lure you into the pit
with this neighborly little drop.
The ugly transformation begins a
second or two after you get to your
feet. when the wave starts to look like a
Nicaraguan hotel in an 8.0 earthquake. Marvin Foster
surfs Pipe enough to know that friendly faces don't always tell the
truth. Sequence: Don King/Lightwaves.

opposite:
Industry Sans Serif Bold. USA, 1991

Circa 91. Poster/flyer. Application of Industry
The Museum of Contemporary Art, USA, 1991
Design Barry Deck

A Benefit for
the Museum of Contemporary Art

The New Group
of the Museum of Contemporary Art
PRESENTS

CIRCA
91
An Evening of Performance Art
Friday, June 7, 1991
8:00 to 11:00 p.m.
CABARET METRO
AND SMART BAR
3730 North Clark Street

FEATURING

KAREN FINLEY

ANDY SOMA

LAWRENCE STEGER

BRENDAN deVALLANCE

NANCY FOREST BROWN

IRIS MOORE

Live musical entertainment by
BIG HAT

AND

MAESTRO SUBGUM
AND THE WHOLE

1. Karen Finley
2. Brendan deVallance
3. Nancy Forest Brown
4. Big Hat
5. Maestro Subgum and the Whole

Hear recorded excerpts from "Works in Progress"
by Los Angeles radio performance artist
JOE FRANK

OPEN BAR UNTIL 11PM

MCA

Hours:
Gallery: Tuesday-Saturday 11:00-5:00, Sunday 12:00-5:00 Office: Monday-Friday 10:00-6:00

Y·O·U·R
N·A·M·E
H·E·R·E

LACE is supported in part by
Art Matters Inc., Border Grill,
FilmForum continues its
CITY, the California Arts Coun-
programming in the LACE
cil, Community Redevelopment
Performance Space. For
Agency of the City of Los Ange-
further information call
les, Cultural Affairs Depart-
[213] 276-7452.
ment of the City of Los Angeles,
the James Irvine Foundation,
S.K. Kojima and Co., L.A. Eyeworks,
Meet the Composer, MIKA Com-
pany, the National Endowment
for the Arts, Norton Family
Foundation, Proton Corporation,
Rockefeller Foundation,
Yamaha International, and the
FRIENDS and SUPPORTERS of LACE.

Non-profit
U. S. Postage
Paid
Permit #33621
Los Angeles, CA

September 89
213.624.5690
Los Angeles, CA 90021
1804 Industrial Street
Los Angeles Contemporary Exhibitions

STAFF
Anne Bray, Video Coordinator
Erica Bornstein, Performance Coordinator
Danae Falliers, Acting Development Coordinator
Laurie Garris, Acting Director
Jinger Heffner, Exhibitions Coordinator
Deborah King, Administrative Assistant
Jane Leslie, Bookkeeper   **INTERNS/VOLUNTEERS**
Dan Bernier, Bookstore Manager
June Scott, Development Assistant   Brian Baltin, Naomi Putterman/Performance Interns
Joy Silverman, Executive Director   Caroline Czirr/Video Intern
                                     Alyssa Resnick/Exhibitions Intern
                                     Sarah Vogwill/Bookstore Intern

MEMBERSHIP

_____ **MEMBER $50**
Receives the LACE bi-monthly calendar with advance
notice and invitations to all openings. 10% discount at
the LACE Bookstore. Members-only discount to LACE
performances, and with select Los Angeles merchants.

_____ **FAN $100**
Receives all of the above PLUS one LACE publication.

_____ **FRIEND of LACE $250**
Receives all of the above PLUS your name in lights on
our illuminated, digital display, PLUS invitations to
attend at least two exceptional events which highlight
noteworthy people and ideas.

Make checks payable to Los Angeles Contemporary Exhibitions or LACE.

_____ **SUPPORTER $1000**
Receives all the benefits of the FRIENDS, PLUS an invitation
to attend a special Supporters-only Artists' event. PLUS
your name on a permanent earthquake support plate on
the LACE building. Your $1000 contribution literally
"supports" LACE!

_____ **ARTIST/STUDENT/SENIOR MEMBER $20**
Same benefits as Member.

NAME: _____
ADDRESS: _____
CITY/STATE/ZIP: _____
PHONE: _____

SEND TO:
Los Angeles Contemporary Exhibitions
1804 Industrial Street
Los Angeles, CA 90021

LACE NEEDS VOLUNTEERS!

free one-year membership to LACE.
hands-on experience in the process, and a
5650 to volunteer your time and receive
opment techniques. Please call 213 624-
lery and performance production and devel-
portunity to participate in all aspects of gal-
laboratory where volunteers are given the op-
involved in fundraising for LACE! LACE is a
face the challenges of development and get
putting together a visual arts exhibition!
stallation, and gain first-hand experience
performance, the ins and outs of media in-
learn the technical aspects of lighting for

Flyer. Application of Keedy
Los Angeles Contemporary Exhibitions, USA, 1989

opposite top: *Keedy Sans Bold.* USA, 1989

opposite: *Hard Times Regular.* USA, 1990

Design Jeffery Keedy

ABCDEFGH
abcdefgh
IJKLMNOPQ
ijklmnopq
RSTUVWXYZ
rstuvwxyz
1234567890

ABCDEFGH
abcdefgh
IJKLMNOPQ
ijklmnopq
RSTUVWXYZ
rstuvwxyz
1234567890

F State. UK, 1991

opposite: Application of F State. State poster. FontShop, UK, 1991. Design Neville Brody

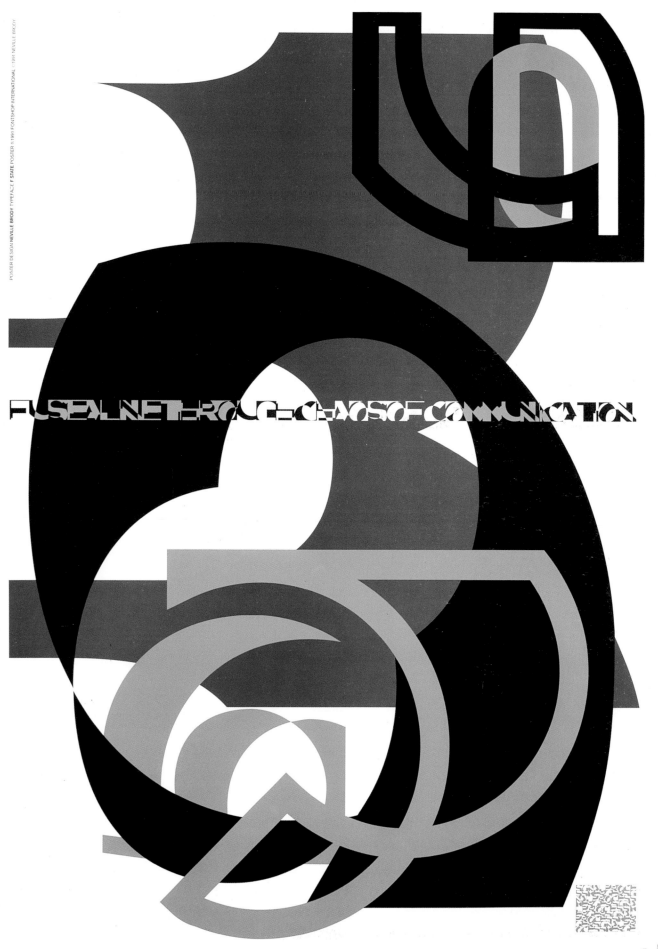

POSTER DESIGN **NEVILLE BRODY** TYPEFACE **F STATE** POSTER ©1991 FONTSHOP INTERNATIONAL ©1991 NEVILLE BRODY

FUSEALNETHROUGHECHAOSOFCOMMUNICATION.

index

159.5mm

" NOW THAT'S WHAT I CALL TYPOGRAPHY. VOLUME ONE. "